FROM MY COLD DEAD FINGERS

Gerald,

in freedom,

Richard J. Mark

Other books by Richard I. Mack:

Government, God and Freedom:
A Fundamental Trinity

The Proper Role of Law Enforcement:
What Every Citizen Should Know,
What Every Cop Should Believe

FROM MY COLD DEAD FINGERS

Why America Needs Guns

Sheriff Richard I. Mack

RAWHIDE
WESTERN
PUBLISHING

First Edition copyright Timothy Robert Walters and Richard I. Mack,
September 1994
Second printing, October 1994
Third printing, February 1995

Second (Revised) Edition copyright Timothy Robert Walters and Richard I.
Mack, April 1996
Second printing, Revised Edition, February 1998

Third Edition ("Final Chapter") copyright Richard I. Mack, May 2000

Cover design: Vance Hawkins
Cover model: Dawn Mack
Front and back cover photography: Dale Holladay, Safford, Arizona
Printed by MC Printing, Provo, Utah

Mack, Richard I., 1952
        From My Cold Dead Fingers : Why America Needs Guns (update)
America / Richard I. Mack. 3rd ed.

        Includes bibliographical references and index.

        ISBN 0-9641935-4-X : $14.95

        Library of Congress Catalog Card Number : 96-68098

Acknowledgements

A work such as this is never done solely by its author. Thank God for those who went before us, blazing trails through mountains of information and paving the way for latter-day researchers. A heartfelt "thank you" is hereby extended to David B. Kopel, Director of the Second Amendment Project at the Independence Institute in Golden, Colorado; to Paul H. Blackman, Ph.D., of the National Rifle Association's Institute for Legislative Action; to Gary Kleck, researcher, author, and criminologist at Florida State University; to W. Cleon Skousen, author, mentor, former FBI administrator, and former Salt Lake City chief of police; and to Larry Pratt of the Gun Owners Foundation.

Thanks also to all those who shared their stories and their lives with us, especially Jesse Peterson and Dr. Suzie Gratia.

Sufficient personal gratitude cannot be expressed for the time, and moral support—not to mention other kinds of cooperation—provided by my attorney, David T. Hardy, and by my bride, Dawn Mack, and my children. I must also acknowledge the invaluable moral support from my parents, G. Wayne and Ruth Mack, and all those defenders of constitutional liberty who bought pre-publication copies of this book, enabling its timely production.

The Federal Government may neither issue directives requiring the States to address particular problems, nor command the States' officers, or those of their political subdivisions, to administer or enforce a federal regulatory program. It matters not whether policy making is involved, and no case-by-case weighing of the burdens of benefits is necessary; such commands are fundamentally incompatible with our constitutional system of dual sovereignty.

—Justice Antonin Scalia,
United States Supreme Court ruling
in *Mack* v. *U.S.*, June 27, 1997

DEDICATION

For Dawn,
Joshua, Rich, Jimmy, Luci, and Mandie

... and those who would fight
to keep them free.

In Memory
of
Dyan Holguin
(1952-1994)
and
Jimmy Waite
(1952-1994)

Contents

Part I:
Vigilantes and Victims

Contents

Part II:
Fallacies and Facts

Foreword Message

"No man thinks more highly than I do of ... patriotism. ... But different men often see the same subject in different lights; and, therefore, I hope it will not be thought disrespectful ... if ... I should speak forth my sentiments freely, and without reserve. This is no time for ceremony. The question ... is one of awful moment to this country. Should I keep back my opinions at such time through fear of giving offense, I should consider myself guilty of treason towards my country, and of an act of disloyalty towards my country, and of an act of disloyalty towards the majesty of heaven, which I revere above all things.

"... [I]t is natural to man to indulge in the illusions of hope. We are apt to shut our eyes against a painful truth, and listen to the song of that siren, till she transforms us into beasts. Is this the part of wise men engaged in a great and arduous struggle for liberty? Are we disposed to be of the number of those who having eyes, see not, and having ears, hear not, the things which so nearly concern their temporal salvation? For my part, whatever anguish of spirit it may cost, I am willing to know the whole truth; to know the worst, and to provide for it.

"I have but one lamp by which my feet are guided, and that is the lamp of experience. I know of no way of judging the future but by the past. And judging by the past, I wish to know what there has been … to justify [the] hopes with which gentlemen have been pleased to solace themselves …? Is it that insidious smile with which our petition has been lately received? Trust it not, sir; it will prove a snare to your feet. Suffer not yourselves to be betrayed with a kiss. Ask yourselves how this gracious reception … comports with those warlike preparations which cover our waters and darken our land. … Let us not deceive ourselves. … These are the implements of war and subjugation—the last arguments to which kings resort. I ask … what means this martial array if its purpose be not to force us to submission? Can gentlemen assign any other possible motive for it? … And what have we to oppose them? Shall we try argument? Sir, we have been trying that for ten years last. Have we anything new to offer upon the subject? Nothing. We have held the subject up in every light of which was capable; but it has been all in vain. Shall we resort to entreaty and humble supplication? Let us not … deceive ourselves longer. Sir, we have done everything that could be done to divert the storm which is now coming on.

"We have petitioned; we have remonstrated; we have supplicated; we have prostrated ourselves before the throne, and have implored its interposition. … Our petitions have been slighted; our remonstrances have produced additional violence and insult; our supplications have been disregarded; and we have been spurned, with contempt, from the foot of the throne. In vain, after these things, we may indulge the fond hope of peace and reconciliation. There is no longer any room for hope. If we wish to be free; if we mean to preserve inviolate those inestimable privileges for which we have been so long contending; if we mean not basely to abandon the noble struggle in which we have been so long engaged, and which we have pledged ourselves never to abandon until the glorious object of our contest shall be obtained; we must fight! I repeat, sir, we must fight! An appeal to arms and the God of Hosts is all that is left us!

"They tell us ... that we are weak—unable to cope with so formidable an adversary. But when shall we be stronger? Will it be next week or next year? Will it be when we are totally disarmed, and when a ... guard shall be stationed in every house? Shall we gather strength by irresolution and inaction? Shall we acquire the means of effectual resistance by lying supinely on our backs and hugging the delusive phantom of hope until our enemies shall have bound us hand and foot?

"Sir, we are not weak if we make a proper use of those means the God of Nature hath placed in our power. ... [M]illions of people armed in the holy cause of liberty, and in such a country as that which we possess, are invincible by any force which our enemy can send us. Besides, sir, we shall not fight our battles alone. There is a just God who presides over the destinies of nations, and who will raise up friends to fight our battles for us. The battle, sir, is not [to] the strong alone; it is to the vigilant, the active, the brave. Besides, sir, we have no election. If we base enough to desire it, it is now too late to retire from the contest. There is no retreat, but in submission and slavery! Our chains are forged. Their clanking may be heard on the plains of Boston! The war is inevitable—and let it come! I repeat, sir, let it come!

"It is in vain ... to extenuate the matter. Gentlemen may cry "peace, peace," but there is no peace. The war is actually begun! The next gale that sweeps from the north will bring to our ears the clash of resounding arms! Our brethren are already in the field! Why stand we here idle? What is it the gentlemen wish? What would they have? Is life so dear, or peace so sweet, as to [be] purchased at the price of chains and slavery? Forbid it, Almighty God! I know not what course others may take; but as for me, give me liberty or give me death!"

—Patrick Henry (1736-1799)
*spoken before an assembly
of fellow countrymen,
March 1775*

Preface

On February 28, 1994—in a move to keep my oath to serve the people of Graham County, Arizona, and my oath to uphold and defend the U.S. Constitution and the Constitution of the State of Arizona—I filed a lawsuit in Federal District Court in Tucson, Arizona, to fight the enactment of the Brady Bill.

Since the very first mention of the Brady Bill, I've been against it. A five-day waiting period? *What a ridiculous nuisance,* I thought. I knew a waiting period would violate the Second Amendment *and* the Arizona Constitution's guarantee that citizens' rights to keep and bear arms could not be "impaired," but I waited to see the actual bill before I passed final judgment.

In January, the Bureau of Alcohol, Tobacco and Firearms (BATF) sent us (all law enforcement administrators) copies of *their* interpretation of the Brady Bill, and instructions detailing our "duties" to enforce it. The BATF followed up by meeting with all county attorneys and sheriffs in Arizona on February 2, 1994, and again discussed with us means by which we would be enforcing the Brady Bill. Every sheriff and county attorney present was opposed to the Brady Bill; not one of us felt it would help curb the tide of violence and crime in Arizona or any place else. I decided at that time I would have to fight the Brady Bill or succumb to the pressure to violate my oath of office by serving the Federal Government instead of the people of Graham County.

The next day—February 3, 1994—I called the National Rifle Association and asked to speak to a legal advisor. I spoke with Mr. Richard Gardiner. I asked him if I could sue the federal government in order to stop the implementation of the Brady Bill. Gardiner said I could, and the NRA would help me prepare the paperwork. Eventually, the paperwork was prepared by NRA lawyers and my own attorney, David T. Hardy. The suit was filed the day the Brady Bill took effect.

My opposition to the Brady Bill was three-fold:

First, the law is completely contrary to the U.S. Constitution—i.e., the Second Amendment (the right to keep and bear arms); the Tenth Amendment (states' rights); the Thirteenth Amendment (involuntary servitude); and the Fourteenth Amendment (violating privileges and immunities of citizens and due process). The Brady Bill also violates the Constitution of Arizona, which states, "... *the rights of the individual citizen to keep and bear arms in his own defense or in defense of the state, shall not be impaired.*"

I have sworn an oath in the name of God to uphold and defend both the U.S. and Arizona Constitutions. How could I enforce the Brady Handgun Control Law and keep my oath of office?

Second, the Federal Government has no jurisdictional authority to order or command me (or any other sheriff in this country) to enforce *federal* law. There are 53 different federal law enforcement entities whose employees have been hired to enforce federal law. I am not a federal agent; I work for Graham County and was hired by the people of the county to do their bidding. This is what Abraham Lincoln was talking about when he said,

"… that this nation, under God, shall have a new birth of freedom, and that government of the people, by the people and for the people, shall not perish from the earth."

Am I a servant of the Federal Government, or of the people of Graham County?

Finally, the Brady Bill imposes a great burden on the limited manpower, budgets and resources of sheriffs' offices. The law would have us spend our time, efforts and resources doing *criminal* background checks on honest, law-abiding citizens. This is not only a ridiculous waste of time, but treats citizens as criminals for merely exercising their Second Amendment rights.

Further, no gun control law—of which there are over 20,000 already—is going to convince criminals to give up their guns. The Brady Bill and 20 more like it will do nothing to stop crime or impede the flow of violence in America.

When public servants—police officers, legislators, and even the President—take a solemn oath to uphold and defend the Constitution, it should become their steadfast mission. Otherwise, the U.S. Constitution becomes a collection of meaningless words in the hands of government officials.

Our Constitution is hanging by a thread. It is our right, it is our *duty*, to make sure the tenets of freedom as proclaimed by our Founding Fathers "shall not perish from the earth."

—Richard I. Mack

Residual state sovereignty was also implicit, of course, in the Constitution's conferral upon Congress of not all governmental powers, but only discrete and enumerated ones.

—Justice Antonin Scalia
in *Mack* v. *U.S.* Supreme Court ruling

Introduction

On June 28, 1994, U.S. District Judge John Roll ruled on Sheriff Richard Mack's lawsuit challenging the constitutionality of the Brady Handgun Law. He wrote:

> The Court finds that in enacting section 18 U.S.C. 922(s)(2), Congress exceeded its authority under Article 1, section 8 of the United States Constitution, thereby impermissibly encroaching upon the powers retained by the states pursuant to the Tenth Amendment. The Court further finds that the provision, in conjunction with the criminal sanctions its violation would engender, is unconstitutionally vague under the Fifth Amendment of the United States Constitution.

Other sheriffs, following Sheriff Mack's lead, filed similar lawsuits. A federal judge in Montana—ruling in a suit filed by Sheriff Jay Printz—said §922(s)(2) of the Brady Bill was unconstitutional. In another suit, a judge in Mississippi agreed. A federal judge in Texas, however, ruled in favor of the Brady Act.

It's interesting to note, within two weeks of Judge Roll's decision, the U.S. Justice Department and the U.S. Attorney's office in Arizona implored the court to rewrite the ruling so it would apply to only Sheriff Mack. (The Mississippi decision applies only to Sheriff McGee, who filed the challenge). It seems as though our "Pledge of Allegiance" (… with liberty and justice for all) has taken a one-way hike down Memory Lane. Perhaps that oath was not meant to affect the Justice Department.

On July 11, 1995, Sheriffs Mack of Arizona and Printz of Montana saw their lawsuits overturned by a three-judge panel in the Ninth U.S. Circuit Court of Appeals in San Francisco. The decision came on a two-to-one split vote.

Justice Canby wrote for the majority: "… *there is likely to be some point at which a federal statute that enlists the aid of state employees can become so burdensome to the state that it violates the Tenth Amendment. … We conclude, however, that the Brady Act does not approach that point.*" It would appear, then, in the view of Judge Canby and at least one of his colleagues, that it's okay to be a little unconstitutional, as long as the offense is not too flagrant.

Interestingly, however, Justice Fernandez (a Bill Clinton appointee) cast the dissenting vote. He wrote: "*This case makes palpable the notion that the states are just a part of the national government, a notion that was rejected when this country was founded. … [T]he Federal Government may not compel the states to enact or administer a federal regulatory program. … The time to stop this journey of a thousand miles is at the first step.*"

Largely, government officials and agencies no longer respect common citizens trying to live within their constitutional guarantees. Too many freedoms are being perpetually destroyed by an out-of-control government whose job it is to protect individual, God-given rights.

A crusade in this country has begun, and numerous citizens are joining the "holy cause of liberty." Several federal judges sided with the seven sheriffs who ultimately filed challenges against the Brady Bill. The Fifth Circuit Court of Appeals also agreed with the sheriffs based on the Tenth Amendment.

Finally, Sheriff Printz and Sheriff Mack appeared before the United States Supreme Court, and on June 27, 1997, the Supreme Court declared the Brady Bill to be unconstitutional. In a 5-4 split decision, Justice Scalia delivered the opinion of the court. "But the Constitution protects us from our own best intentions," Scalia reminded Congress. (Wouldn't it be amazing if Congress actually paid attention to this principle?) Justice Scalia warned and reminded us all that the states are not subject to federal direction.

This decision, perhaps the most powerful and monumental Tenth-amendment ruling in the history of our country, has opened the door to the individual states and local governments to escape the heavy hand of federal intrusiveness. Now, it will take governors, state legislators, city councils, school boards, county commissioners, and law enforcement authorities who have the guts to walk through the door.

The reaction from President Clinton, gun-control advocate Sarah Brady and mainstream media to the Brady Bill being found unconstitutional was typically liberal. They said the Supreme Court ruling was "meaningless."

This ruling was truly miraculous. More miracles are needed as we, the people, wake up and join those who have had the courage to stand for constitutional American liberty.

—David T. Hardy

A well regulated Militia, being necessary to the security of a free State, the right of the people to keep and bear Arms, shall not be infringed.

—U.S. Constitution, Second Amendment

I

Vigilantes
and
Victims

From My Cold Dead Fingers

When they take MY gun, they'll pry it from my cold, dead fingers.

—an American sentiment

Subway Self-defense

He'd been mugged before.

It happened in 1981. In a New York subway three youths jumped him, apparently attracted by some electronic equipment he carried. Somehow, interest in the coveted items was lost in the violent attempt to take them. The muggers saw their thin, nondescript victim as an easy target. They began pushing him around, then threw him to the floor. In a desperate struggle to escape, he regained his feet and was brutally slammed into a glass door. The breath went out of him as the door handle rammed into his chest. He was bleeding and he thought he would be killed.

Someone came to his aid and helped subdue one of the attackers. The others ran away. Electronic equipment lay scattered and broken. For six hours the mugging victim was detained at the train station and questioned by police. The accused mugger was released in half that time. Ultimately, a charge of criminal mischief was brought against the attacker because he had allegedly torn his victim's jacket.

So this was how the New York system of criminal justice worked. Plagued by fear and constant pain in his damaged knees, the mugging victim bought a gun. He invested a good deal of effort, time and money into preparing the proper forms and applications for a concealed weapons license. A desk officer at NYPD summarily denied his request. Frustrated by a stone wall of bureaucratic apathy, Bernhard Goetz decided to carry the weapon anyway.[1]

The decision brought him comfort in his daily activities. On one occasion while walking near Central Park, he discouraged another mugging by simply pulling and displaying the weapon. No one could have guessed, however, that a quiet man's desire for self-protection would catapult him to national folk hero status and cost him years of personal agony.

The precipitating event occurred three days before Christmas in 1984. Goetz left his apartment on 14th Street and walked to the IRT Station at the corner of 7th Avenue. He entered a subway car occupied by a group of passengers huddled at one end and four rowdy black youths at the other. He sat down between the two groups.

One of the youths said, "How are ya?"

A bell went off in Goetz's head. He recalled his friend Al, the doorman at Courtney House on 14th. Al had been mugged and severely beaten during an encounter that began with his attacker uttering blandly, "How are you doing?"

Two of the young men pressed toward the slight figure of Bernhard Goetz sitting quietly in dungarees and windbreaker. They asked for money. Goetz asked them to repeat what they wanted. They demanded five dollars. In the brief seconds that followed, Goetz fired five shots from a Smith & Wesson revolver, and three rowdy black youths went down, crying and bleeding. The fourth sat paralyzed on the car seat, his spine severed.

---

[1] *A Crime of Self Defense*, George P. Fletcher, The Free Press, A division of Macmillan, Inc., New York, NY, 1988, pp. 12-13.

The train lurched to a halt. A conductor asked Goetz if he was a cop. Goetz paused to comfort two terrified female passengers kneeling to pray. Empty pistol still in hand, he went to the platform outside the car, dropped the safety chain and lost himself in the shadows of the subway tunnel.

For nine days the "mysterious gunman" dropped out of sight. Police worked feverishly to locate him. The media had a field day with video footage of the four wounded teenagers and much speculation on the "subway vigilante." Overwhelming sentiment favoring a would-be victim who stood up to unlikely odds and served a helping of common man's justice spread like windswept flame across the nation. After several days of reflection (and fear of apprehension by police) in the quieter milieu of Vermont and New Hampshire, Goetz walked into a police station at Concord prepared to face the music.[2]

Goetz was praised as a hero by the common citizenry of New York and the rest of the country. However, officials condemned him as a menace who would dare to assume the responsibility of public safety generally assigned to trained police. Mayor Ed Koch spoke adamantly about "vigilantism," and President Reagan referred to the "breakdown of civilization." The NAACP called Goetz a 21st-century Ku Klux Klan "nightrider." Authorities fearful of a sudden rash of vigilante actions defended by claims of self-defense decided to make an example of Bernhard Hugo Goetz. After grand jury hearings, appeals and rulings amounting to two years of preparation, Goetz was brought to trial on 13 counts ranging from attempted murder and assault to the unlawful possession of a firearm.[3]

---

[2] *A Crime of Self Defense*, George P. Fletcher, pp. 1-4, 11.
[3] *A Crime of Self Defense*, George P. Fletcher, p. 4.

Two and a half years after that fateful afternoon on the IRT train, a jury found Goetz guilty on one count of criminal possession of a weapon in the third degree. He was acquitted on two counts of criminal possession of a weapon in the fourth degree, four charges of attempted murder and six other related charges.[4]

In response to the verdict some black political and social leaders cried "racism," forgetting that one of the women Goetz had comforted as he left the train was black. Those more concerned with the civil rights of four black hoodlums than the safety of innocent subway passengers deliberately omitted references to the youths' previous arrest records and the screwdrivers they carried as potential weapons. A full decade after the dramatic subway shooting, the legal and moral debate continues.

When does an individual cross the line between using force to protect oneself and using *deadly* force to protect oneself? Do four strapping aggressors against one frail victim constitute justification for use of a deadly weapon? Must a mugging victim see an aggressor's concealed screwdriver before taking defensive action any more than a rape victim must see the "weapon" that will penetrate, maim and defile before shooting the would-be rapist? Has the cry of "racism" become a standard cop-out, a universal rationalization of decadent behavior among aimless young blacks anytime a white person gets the upper hand? Have we as a society become so police-state oriented, statute regulated and civil-rights indoctrinated that someone must be killed, injured or deprived of property before *anybody* can do *anything* to alter the course of events?

---

[4] *A Crime of Self Defense*, George P. Fletcher, p. 198.

In the case of Bernhard Goetz and the four black youths on the subway train, there should never have been an arrest. There should have been no charges filed against a man protecting himself in the face of obvious threat and overwhelming odds. There should never have been a jury selected, a trial held, or the need for a single conviction of any kind—all at enormous expense to the taxpayers of New York. There should never have been a debate—moral or legal.

Bernhard Goetz was threatened. He recognized the danger he was in. He defended himself and avoided becoming a statistic buried in some annual NYPD report on unsolved violent crime. He did not spark a tidal wave of copycat vigilante incidents across the nation. That's because responsible Americans saw his actions as those of a responsible American under threat of personal harm or injury. It just so happened that Bernhard Goetz had a gun.

And so it was intended by the Founding Fathers of the United States of America.

The Constitution shall never be construed to prevent the people of the United States who are peaceable citizens from keeping their own arms.

—Samuel Adams

Founding Fathers' Intent

They wrote simply, "... *the right of the people to keep and bear Arms, shall not be infringed.*"[5]

That's all it says because that's exactly what the framers of the Constitution wanted to say. The Bill of Rights—within which the above provision comprises half of the Second Amendment—was written to calm the expressed fears of some opponents of the Constitution as it was originally presented. Some members of Congress expressed concern that the national government would ultimately try to exercise too much control over the states and the people therein. Other statesmen argued that a Bill of Rights was moot because the federal government would *never* have the power to do the things expressly forbidden in the original ten amendments.

Nonetheless, for the sake of a document too good to be threatened by a lack of consensus, the Bill of Rights was drafted in 1789 and ratified by the individual states two years later. Its separate amendments were intended exactly as they were written, with no exceptions, stipulations, conditions or arguments. ... *the right of the people to keep and bear Arms, shall not be infringed.*

---

[5] U.S. Constitution, Bill of Rights, Second Amendment.

It came as the result of previous oppressive government behavior and couldn't have been written any plainer.

During the early stages of American history, tension grew between the colonists and the British government. American leaders tried for more than a decade to find peaceful solutions to the issues between the Colonies and Britain. However, their attempts were consistently spurned by King George III. In 1776, the British Parliament empowered itself with the right to legislate for the Colonies in all matters. Colonists focused their main opposition on excessive taxation, but other acts by the British government were also declared intolerable acts like quartering soldiers in private homes, excessive fines, cruel and unusual punishments, forced allegiance to the Church of England, the absence of a free press, and *gun control.*

When British troops confiscated a colonial arsenal in September of 1774, some 60,000 patriots took up arms in defense of their neighbors and country. A few months later in perhaps his most famous address, Patrick Henry said, "... a well regulated militia, composed of gentlemen and freemen, is the natural strength and only security of a free government."[6]

This principle of freedom referred to by Patrick Henry was true in 1775; it is true today, and it will be true tomorrow and always. Indeed, we as Americans owe our liberty and freedom to the brave and determined colonists and "minutemen" who armed themselves with their own guns and risked their lives to fight the tyranny of King George III. The American Republic would not exist today had it not been for a conviction among the early patriots that they had a right to keep and bear arms.

---

[6] *The Right to Keep and Bear Arms*, Report of the Committee on the Judiciary, United States Senate, U.S. Government Printing Office, Washington, D.C., 1982, p. 4.

The United States of America did not gain its independence on July 4, 1776, as commonly celebrated. This was the day independence was *declared*, one year after the Revolutionary War began, and approximately seven years before it ended on September 3, 1783.

The colonists' victory in this revolution was nothing short of a miracle. These poorly equipped and badly disorganized countrymen effectively defeated the greatest and most powerful empire in the world. However, this first "miracle" only set the stage for an even greater accomplishment to follow as the Founding Fathers set about bringing a new nation together under a virgin national government.

Complete independence was recognized by Britain at the signing of the Treaty of Paris in September of 1783. Thus was born the burden of developing a new government. Some of the 13 states wanted to form a union. Others wished to remain separate and sovereign, fearing a recurrence of tyranny from an all-powerful central government.

There was little unity between the states as they wandered aimlessly through the caverns of their new-found freedoms. Disagreements over commerce, taxes and governmental controls nearly caused another war. Finally, in May of 1787, a Constitutional Convention was organized, and delegates from 12 states met in Philadelphia to establish the United States Constitution. (Rhode Island boycotted the Convention, still fearing possible government domination.)

After 16 months of arduous debate, 39 of the 55 constitutional delegates ratified the Constitution. There was still some very strong opposition, however. New York, Virginia, North Carolina and Rhode Island refused to ratify the Constitution unless it included a Bill of Rights. Opponents to the carefully crafted document felt it needed to specifically detail certain rights the government absolutely could not touch, alter or infringe. Patrick Henry was one of the most ardent proponents of a Bill of Rights.

Initially, there were a staggering 189 amendments recommended for inclusion in the list of "safeguards" outlined by concerned statesmen. Congress approved only 12 of them. The states ratified the ten basic rights the Founding Fathers had determined were the most vital in guaranteeing freedom and liberty to the citizens of a nation. These were the fundamental principles of freedom that were *never* to be violated by their entrusted guardian—the Federal Government.

For 200 years the Bill of Rights has proven to be a sage and unshakable blueprint for freedom. In 1982, the U.S. Senate Judiciary Committee released a report on the Second Amendment. It said, "Together with freedom of the press, the right to keep and bear arms became one of the individual rights most prized by the colonists."

The U.S. Constitution and the Bill of Rights were established as a result of tyrannical usurpations by Britain. The Founding Fathers wanted to guarantee that future governmental officials would not repeat the despotic actions of the past.

Founding Father Richard Henry Lee said, "To preserve liberty, it is essential that the whole body of the people always possess arms, and be taught alike, especially when young, how to use them."[7]

Lee's colleague, statesman Samuel Adams, added, "The said Constitution shall never be construed to authorize Congress

---

[7] *The Right to Keep and Bear Arms*, Committee on the Judiciary, United States Senate, p. vii.

to prevent the people of the United States who are peaceable citizens from keeping their own arms."[8]

Some states held out stubbornly against ratifying the Constitution. It was a long-fought agreement on the first ten amendments that inspired final approval of the Bill of Rights as a part of the U.S. Constitution in December, 1791.

There was little, if any, debate over the Second Amendment. The basic freedom and "unalienable" right to keep and bear arms received unanimous approval. The Founding Fathers considered freedom of religion, freedom of the press, freedom of speech, the right to assemble peaceably, and the right to petition government for a redress of grievances as self-evident and God-given rights. These indisputable tenets of freedom are all included in the First Amendment, and they received more discussion and debate than the right to keep and bear arms. To consider excluding any of these rights from the Constitution would threaten the very concept of American freedom.

Some confusion has existed regarding the reference in the Second Amendment to a "well regulated militia." Militia was defined by the Founding Fathers as *every able-bodied male*, and had absolutely nothing to do with the army or a national guard. The Second Amendment right to keep and bear arms is the right of an individual to possess and carry firearms. This concept is in full accord with the history of the United States of America, and accurately reflects the sentiments of its founding statesmen.

"The conclusion is thus inescapable that the history, concept, and the wording of the Second Amendment to the Con-

---

[8] *The Right to Keep and Bear Arms*, Committee on the Judiciary, United States Senate, p. 5.

stitution of the United States, as well as its interpretation by every major commentator and court in the first half-century after its ratification, indicates that what is protected is an individual right of a private citizen to own and carry firearms in a peaceful manner."[9]

The conclusion *is* inescapable. The Founding Fathers of this nation meant for Congress, the President, and all governmental authorities, *never* to infringe on the rights of the people to keep and bear arms.

---

[9] *The Right to Keep and Bear Arms*, Committee on the Judiciary, United States Senate, p. 12.

The local or municipal authorities form distinct and inde-pendent portions of the supremacy, no more subject ... to the general authority than the general authority is sub-ject to them ....

—James Madison

From My Cold Dead Fingers

It is a natural right which the people have reserved for themselves, confirmed by their Bill of Rights, to keep arms for their own defense.

—New York Journal Supplement

A Legal Act of Murder

They wanted him to work for them, and they devised a plan they thought would leave him no choice.

Randall Weaver—a family man in his early forties—was a man who simply wanted to be left alone, especially by government. He had served his country with honor as a Green Beret during the Vietnam War. He had no criminal record and was not considered a threat to anyone. For the most part, he wanted to live in peace with his wife Vicki and their children—a son Sammy, and daughters Sara and Rachel.

In October of 1989, Randy Weaver sold two shotguns to a man he believed was his friend. The man asked Weaver to cut off the muzzles of the common H&R single-barrel and Remington pump as short as he could. Weaver did so, and the man was on his way … straight to the Bureau of Alcohol, Tobacco and Firearms (BATF), where he worked as an undercover informant.

Some months later a couple of BATF agents approached Weaver with an offer to keep him out of jail if he agreed to spy on a white supremacist group calling itself "Aryan Nations." The man who just wanted to be left alone declined the agents' confusing arrangement, and found himself slapped with an indictment on weapons charges alleging the shotguns he'd sold his "friend" were one-fourth of an inch shorter than legally allowed.[10]

Randy Weaver said to hell with all the bureaucratic trickery and legal complications (or so he thought) and became even more reclusive in the mountains of northern Idaho. His family and young friend Kevin Harris lived in a plywood shack in the woods on Ruby Ridge. They hunted for game, raised garden vegetables and sold firewood for a living. Weaver did not appear for trial. Federal authorities claimed Weaver was trafficking in firearms, and a federal warrant was issued for his arrest.[11]

For nearly a year and a half, then, federal agents staked out the Weavers' mountain cabin. The U.S. Government spent $13,000 a week on an operation to monitor the activities of the Weaver family. A surveillance crew of federal agents hid out in the north woods of Idaho. They wore camouflage outfits with masks across their faces. Their equipment included specialized two-way radios for quiet operation, infrared goggles, semi-automatic handguns, military machine guns, and an HK submachine gun with silencer.[12]

The operation became a high-level media event. Authorities described Weaver as a racist and criminal. They said he was anti-Semitic because of his religious and political views. While his only crime was the alleged illegal alteration of a firearm (and then, of course, not appearing in court), the media were quick to brand him a "radical extremist," often referring to him as a

---

[10] *American Rifleman*, "The Randy Weaver Case ...," Jim Oliver, Nov. 1993.

[11] *U.S. News & World Report*, "Echoes of the Texas Tragedy," Mark Tharp, May 3, 1993, p. 33.

[12] *American Rifleman*, "The Randy Weaver Case ...," Jim Oliver, Nov. 1993.

"mountain man" or "former Green Beret" wanted on weapons violations, hiding out from federal authorities in the rugged terrain of northern Idaho. They called his plywood shack a "mountain fortress." It became "a bunker" and was ultimately described as "a stronghold protected by a cache of 15 weapons and ammunition capable of piercing armored personnel carriers."

By some oversight, perhaps, nobody had thought to deploy "armored personnel carriers" to Ruby Ridge. Neither had anyone considered knocking on Randy Weaver's door and serving the arrest warrant. At this point Randy Weaver had not demonstrated any behavior to indicate he would physically resist. He simply had not shown up in court. (Interestingly, an official letter sent to Weaver instructed him to appear in federal court on March 20, 1991, and the actual hearing was held *February* 20. Of course, officials justified their subsequent behavior by arguing that Weaver never appeared on the wrong date, either.)

After 16 months and approximately $3,000,000 spent, U.S. Marshal William Degan of the Special Operations Group (the Marshals' national SWAT team) was assigned to resolve the standoff. The U.S. Marshal Service named the drama "Operation Northern Exposure." By now, jets were flying reconnaissance over Ruby Ridge, and aerial photographs were being analyzed by the Defense Mapping Agency. Federal agents had picked sniper perches around the Weaver cabin.

On August 21, 1992, 14-year-old Sammy Weaver and his friend Kevin Harris went hunting. Sammy's dog Striker caught scent of the men hiding in the woods. The dog barked and ran ahead. Sammy and Kevin thought he'd picked up the trail of a deer. They hurried to follow. An unexpected burst of gunfire from a hidden sniper stopped Striker in his tracks.

Terrified and confused, Sammy fired his rifle, then turned to flee. A federal agent shot him in the back, killing him instantly. Kevin Harris fired into the woods, mortally wounding Marshal Degan. In the dark of night, Harris and Randy Weaver brought Sammy's body from the woods to a shed near the house.

At the same time, the Weaver property was being surrounded by an army of agents from the BATF, the FBI, the U.S. Marshal Service, Idaho state police, local law enforcement and the Idaho National Guard. Deputy marshals had lied again, claiming the mountain family had them "pinned down" for eight hours when Degan was killed. Gene Glenn, the agent now in charge, said he considered Weaver's kids "hostages." Richard Rogers, head of the FBI's hostage rescue team, ordered a change in the prescribed rules of engagement for FBI sharpshooters that would allow agents to "neutralize" any adult "in the compound."

Randy Weaver did not fully comprehend the odds as they were stacked against him. No one had made any effort to contact Weaver in the capacity of a "negotiator" or other authority.

Weaver and his 16-year-old daughter, Sara—along with Kevin Harris, who was armed—went to the shed where Sammy lay dead. Two hundred yards away, an FBI sniper took aim and fired. The bullet caught Randy Weaver in the arm. The trio bolted for the cabin. Vicki Weaver stood in the doorway, holding her infant daughter Elisheba. Sniper Lon Horiuchi shot her in the face. Some fragments of bullet and of Vicki Weaver's skull wounded Kevin Harris. For a week the family and Harris holed up inside the cabin. Sarah Weaver crawled over her mother's body to prepare food and water for her wounded father and Harris, her 10-year-old sister Rachel and baby Elisheba. FBI negotiators outside taunted the family with remarks like, "How's the baby,

Mrs. Weaver?" and, "Good morning, Randall. How'd you sleep? We're having pancakes. What are you having?"

Kevin Harris came out on August 30. He was whisked off to a Spokane hospital, and charged with the "murder" of Marshal Degan. The Weaver family came out the next day.

The media loved it. They reported Vicki Weaver was killed during a "gun battle." They showed footage of Randy Weaver face down in the road as agents applied handcuffs. Weaver's "arsenal" of weapons, displayed by agents for the television cameras, turned out to be smaller and less impressive than what most farmers keep in their coat closets. For a few days the evening news had a special excitement. But it was all about to end.

Court juries have a built-in mechanism that keeps them from being stupid—or too impulsive. There are usually twelve people involved. The numbers alone serve as a means of check-and-balance within the unit. Emotion is balanced with logic. Confusion is countered with comprehension. Tricky courtroom phraseology glitters less in the light of truth.

Kevin Harris was acquitted on all charges. After a 36-day trial in U.S. District Court in Boise, Idaho, the eight-woman, four-man jury found Randy Weaver not guilty of eight felony charges—including alteration of the shotguns for an undercover operative who had passed himself off as a friend. Judge Edward Lodge had already thrown out two felonies. Weaver was convicted only of failing to appear in court, and of violating his bail conditions (by not appearing in court).

Randy Weaver's defense attorney Gerry Spence summarized simply, "The crime he committed was not sawing off a shotgun. The crime he committed was refusing to go undercover for ATF." He added, "This is a murder case, but the people who committed the murder are not here in court. ... What are we going to do now about the deaths of Vicki Weaver, a mother who was killed with a baby in her arms, and Sammy Weaver, a boy who was shot in the back?"[13]

Those expecting a proper reckoning of justice in this case were in for a long wait. The federal agencies involved tried to sweep it under the carpet, so to speak, and for good reason. During the trial, the FBI was ordered to provide documents they had deliberately withheld for fear they might aid the defense. Evidence presented by the FBI turned out to be falsified. For prosecutorial misconduct the government was ordered to pay a portion of defense attorneys' fees, and U.S. Prosecutor Ron Howen broke down during an apology Judge Lodge ordered him to deliver in open court. The media, of course, lost interest when evidence was shown that agents (and agencies) had lied throughout the drama, applying their own favorable spin to it all.

The media do not savor the taste of crow. A typical story appearing in *U.S. News & World Report* described federal marshals mounting long-range surveillance, "hoping to lure Weaver away from his heavily armed stronghold." The same report stated as undisputed fact that Kevin Harris and Samuel Weaver spotted U.S. marshals and "gave chase" before Sammy was shot in the back.[14]

It's hard to lean so far in one direction and then redeem yourself when you're shown to be so wrong. The easiest "out" is to ignore the issue, don't talk about it and hope it'll go away. The major media are experts at the technique, as are the federal

---

[13] *American Rifleman*, "The Randy Weaver Case ...," Jim Oliver, Nov. 1993.

[14] *U.S. News & World Report*, "Echoes of the Texas Tragedy," Mike Tharp, May 3, 1993, p. 33.

bureaucracies guilty of assigning themselves too much authority and control.

The agencies involved in the tragedy at Ruby Ridge finally came under fire in 1995—*three years later!* FBI agent Larry Potts, who issued the shoot-to-kill order, had already been promoted to deputy director of his agency. A change of power in Congress, facilitated by the November 1994 elections, brought renewed attention to the incident. Under the chairmanship of Senator Arlen Specter of Pennsylvania, the U.S. Senate Judiciary Subcommittee on Terrorism, Technology and Government Information conducted 14 days of public testimony over a six-week period. The panel of senators heard 60 witnesses and reviewed thousands of documents.

In December of 1995, the Subcommittee released a 156-page report. The senators had concluded that the "firefight" on Ruby Ridge was precipitated by Deputy Federal Marshal Arthur Roderick killing Sammy Weaver's dog. They also determined that Larry Potts' rules of engagement were "inappropriate," and that Lon Horiuchi's killing of Vicki Weaver violated the Constitution. The report further confirmed that previous FBI internal reviews were "... *marred by an internal bias to justify agency conduct rather than to find the truth* ..." and that the FBI Shooting Incident Review Team did a "haphazard job" in concluding that Vicki Weaver had placed herself in harm's way and therefore was "subject to deadly force."

The Subcommittee commended FBI Director Louis Freeh for promulgating a new "uniform policy" on deadly force as a result of the Ruby Ridge affair. Freeh's promotion of Larry Potts, however, drew serious criticism. Responsibility for the incident was placed with many of those involved. In conclusion, the report declared that *"... [T]his country can tolerate mistakes made by people like Randy Weaver; but we cannot accept serious errors by federal law enforcement agencies that needlessly result in human tragedy."*

Lon Horiuchi invoked the Fifth Amendment, as did four other federal agents. Larry Potts was demoted. Randy Weaver and his children received a $3,000,000 settlement. The FBI implemented some reforms, including strict new controls over its Hostage Rescue Team. All the U.S. marshals involved in the incident were cited for valor in early 1996 by the director of their agency. Sadly, although perhaps more importantly, "Ruby Ridge" has become the battle cry for an American public that has lost confidence in the integrity of the U.S. Federal Government.

If guns kill people, then:
* *Pencils misspell words.*
* *Automobiles cause accidents and drunk driving.*
* *Spoons made Rosie O'Donnell fat.*

—Brassroots, Inc.,
Tucson, AZ

I love my country, but I fear my government.

—An American reality

The Responsibility Factor

Attorney Gerry Spence says, "If the government wants to kill you, they'll find ways to kill you."

No one has ever taken responsibility for the meaningless killings of Vicki and Sammy Weaver. These victims were not accidentally caught up in a frantic crossfire. They were cut down by trained marksmen who deliberately took aim and fired. It happened as part of an authorized government operation. In the minds of those involved—from control-driven agency heads to their snipers with smoking guns—*that* makes it a justifiable act. Everybody walks away. An attempt was made to punish Kevin Harris for the killing of Marshal Degan, but who answered for snuffing out the lives of a mother holding her baby and a terrified boy who'd just seen his dog riddled with bullets?

Nobody—absolutely nobody!

The United States Congress has allowed this malady to become a conceptual norm within federal agencies. The Federal Government was never supposed to have this much power.

"The powers not delegated to the United States by the Constitution, nor prohibited by it to the States, are reserved to the States respectively, or to the people." [15]

---

[15] U.S. Constitution, Bill of Rights, Tenth Amendment.

Statesmen from the various states formulated the federal government. They were skeptical and cautious. They *deliberately* limited the powers assigned the entity they were creating out of fear of being consumed and made insignificant by its authority. The documents set forth as the laws of the land were simple, clear and concise. They were made easy to understand and obey. It was meant that they never be questioned, rescinded, altered or tampered with. And they provided a way (a two-thirds majority vote of the people of the sovereign states) to abolish the Federal Government if their brainchild got out of hand.

Perhaps the simplest, most easily understood and least debated (at least in 1789) of all the constitutional amendments is the Second Amendment. It contains 27 carefully crafted words: *"A well regulated Militia, being necessary to the security of a free State, the right of the people to keep and bear Arms, shall not be infringed."* It does not say, "... the right of the people to keep and bear arms as determined by the whim of the U.S. Congress." Nor does it say, "... the right of the people to keep and bear arms pursuant to federal restrictions as lobbied into law by Handgun Control, Inc."

The first half of the Second Amendment is an important element here as well. *"A well regulated Militia, being necessary to the security of a free state ..."* refers largely to individual citizens who are well armed to maintain the freedom of their country. The framers of the Bill of Rights actually referred to organized military units like a national guard as *"select* militia," and applied the broader term "militia" to a "universally armed people."[16] Richard Henry Lee would have run screaming from

---

[16] *The Right to Keep and Bear Arms*, Committee on the Judiciary, U.S. Senate, p. 11.

the whole process had one of the originally proposed 189 amendments read, "... the right of the people to keep and bear arms so long as shotguns are not sawed off and rifles are not automatic and handguns are licensed and 20,000 other restrictions deemed to be necessary by future legislative bodies are obeyed."

Gun control advocates in Congress (and other law-making bodies) would argue that changing times and a more complex societal structure has led to the need for thousands of restrictions being imposed on firearms and those who own them. In fact, most pieces of gun-control legislation include as a preface to the proposed regulation several paragraphs of justification for the proposal. However, it is clearly evident that throughout a long history of municipal councils, state legislatures and federal congresses enacting voluminous tides of firearms restrictions, not a single one of them has ever accomplished its intended end. Sidearms were banned from the streets of Tombstone, Arizona, *before* the shootout at OK Corral. "Tommy" guns were outlawed in response to the gang wars of the Prohibition era. Sawed-off shotguns, "zip" guns, "Saturday night specials" and so-called "assault" weapons have all been made illegal. But crime has *never* decreased. The legality or availability of a particular type of weapon has never prevented a single crime from being committed. Homemade weapons (i.e. "zip" guns and others) are typically as risky for the shooter as for a victim. Nobody is making a case for these, but banning their use did not cause street crime to decline. A total ban on all kinds of firearms would only result in crimes being committed with clubs, knives, dynamite, poisons, tire irons, pointed sticks, kitchen utensils, garden tools and *illegal* firearms.

Not all American lawmakers are gun control advocates. However, the majority who are typically suffer from a couple of chronic "ailments." One such affliction is known simply as "liberalitis." Victims of this epidemic within government do not believe American citizens are capable of living, thinking, doing, providing or caring for themselves. Therefore, government must do it all for them. Welfare, socialized health care, and a thousand other entitlements, make otherwise productive people totally dependent on government. (This validates its existence.) Any distinction between classes must be eliminated. In order to do this, every citizen (except federal lawmakers) would carry an I.D. card (as proposed within the Clinton health care plan in 1994). Free enterprise must be stifled (by rangeland and mining reform, wetlands and other environmental designations, and prohibitive taxes imposed on commodities producers, industrial developers and employers large and small). And firearms must be restricted, regulated, registered and traceable so they may ultimately be confiscated, leaving the common American citizen with no defense against Big Brother. (We will discuss this highly contagious element at some length in subsequent chapters of this book.)

The second malady rampant among Washington "anti-gunners" is the old-school Knee Jerk Syndrome. It is usually precipitated by an inability to learn from past experiences. Sufferers are devoid of practical or innovative thought processes. They're usually lazy and look for an easy way out. The symptoms never change. Drug dealers kill one another, so *let's regulate firearms.* Someone does a report on hunting accidents, so *let's regulate firearms.* Teenage suicides are up, so *let's regulate firearms.* Gang-related crime continues to escalate, so *let's regulate firearms.* Someone shoots at a president, so LET'S REGULATE FIREARMS AND MAKE IT *IMPOSSIBLE* TO SHOOT AT A PRESIDENT AGAIN!

That rationale is stale and ineffective. Gun control has never, and will never, curb the violent behavior of criminals and impassioned offenders. Increased violent crime is but a symptom of a fast-spreading social disease not so very different from leprosy and AIDS in producing an inescapable end result—suffering and death. No social disease will ever be cured by Congress banning merchandise or restricting Americans' rights. Imagine the impact on drug addiction if a law were passed imposing high taxes on medical syringes ... or the reduced spread of AIDS if HIV-positive individuals were banned from having sex. Gun control, as applied to violence and criminal activity, is equally as ludicrous.

Gun control advocates have never been supported by facts—that is, of course, unless you accept their "facts" as substantiated by conjecture, hype, lopsided reports and "adjusted" statistics. Their most effective tool is the ability to frighten an audience with graphic illustrations of innocent people (especially children) maimed and killed with guns. In order to achieve this, however, they must dwell on all things negative, stubbornly ignoring and avoiding the overwhelmingly more positive "truths" of safety, self-protection, crime prevention, free enterprise, sporting activities, predator control, wildlife management, and preserving American freedom. The national media provide an express highway for their tainted message. The most sensational crimes make the biggest headlines. One rotten kid with a blazing Smith & Wesson makes more exciting news than 100,000 good ones doing their homework.

Gun control first became an important national issue in the 1960s. However, there was virtually no data upon which to base any intelligent approach to the matter. In 1978, the Carter Administration—believing the facts would support stringent federal gun regulation—commissioned an extensive study of the effects of firearms upon the American society. President Carter appointed sociology professor James D. Wright and two respected colleagues as a "grant-review team" under the National Institute of Justice. With 20,000 gun control laws on the books across the nation, Wright and his team of sociologists favored much stricter regulations. The grant-review team was specifically instructed to study the issue from the perspective that gun control was good and the country needed more of it. However, in a report delivered to the National Institute of Justice in 1982, the esteemed researchers could document *no evidence* that America's gun control laws had reduced criminal violence.[17]

Specific examples cited included the federal Gun Control Act of 1968. The law banning most interstate gun sales had virtually no effect on criminals obtaining guns from other states. A law in Detroit imposing mandatory sentences for felonies committed with guns had no influence on gun-crime statistics. A ban on ownership of unregistered handguns in Washington, D.C., could not be linked to any reduction in crime.

Further, one of the most detailed studies of gun control results was compiled by Gary Kleck of Florida State University. Kleck, a liberal Democrat actively involved with the Civil Liberties Union, sought information on the impact of nearly 20 different kinds of gun control, and how they affected incidents of suicides, accidents and five different serious crimes. The study was done using data available for the years 1979 to 1981. Waiting periods for obtaining firearms, and all kinds of licensing and registration schemes, had no influence on statistics. Interestingly,

---

[17] *Policy Review,* "The Violence of Gun Control," David B. Kopel, Winter 1993.

Kleck learned that gun control *did* reduce suicides committed with *guns*, but had no effect on the overall suicide rate. Other methods were simply more frequent.[18]

Professor James Wright and Peter Rossi, a professor at the University of Massachusetts and future president of the American Sociology Association, conducted still another study for the National Institute of Justice. From interviews with felons serving time in ten different states, the professors learned that gun control has no effect on criminals obtaining weapons; it doesn't even create an inconvenience. Only seven percent of criminals specializing in handgun crime had armed themselves through a gun store. From that small number, many of the guns were either stolen from stores or purchased by another person with no record. Still others bought their guns legally before acquiring a record.[19]

"Gun control" is a failed concept. It doesn't lend itself to the purported intent (to reduce crime, suicides and accidents)—never has, never will. Still, about 10,000 new gun control measures are proposed each year by persistent lawmakers. There is an active movement afoot to disarm completely and forever the common citizens of the United States.

NBC News President Michael Gartner told *USA Today*, "There is no reason for anyone in this country anyone except a police officer or a military person to buy, to own, to have, to use, a handgun. ... The only way to control handgun use in this

---

[18] *Point Blank: Guns and Violence in America*, Gary Kleck, Aldine de Gruyther, Hawthorne, NY, 1991.

[19] *Policy Review*, "The Violence of Gun Control," David B. Kopel, Winter 1993.

country is to prohibit the guns. And the only way to do that is to change the Constitution."[20]

President Clinton told the same publication, "We can't be so fixated on our desire to preserve the rights of ordinary Americans to legitimately own handguns and rifles ... that we are unable to think about reality."[21]

The United States of America is in serious trouble when its president believes we can't be "fixated" on a desire to preserve the rights of ordinary Americans! The U.S. Constitution and subsequent Bill of Rights were drawn by statesmen worried sick over the "rights of ordinary Americans." And did you notice the President included *rifles* in his visionary statement? The unspoken motivation behind sweeping gun control measures currently being prepared for introduction is not crime reduction or accident prevention. It's an orchestrated effort to disarm a nation.

Think about what they're saying:

"... can't be so fixated on our desire to preserve the rights of ordinary Americans ..."

"... the only way to do that is to change the Constitution."

There are many senators and representatives in Washington with similar sentiments. *They* are the ones who passed the Brady Bill and thousands of other gun-restricting laws contrary to the tenets of the U.S. Constitution. *They* are the ones who have clogged the justice system with ineffective mandates. *They* have chipped away like diligent sculptors at the "rights of ordinary Americans." *They* determined that honest American citizens must *license* the same articles the Founding Fathers made

---

[20] *USA Today*, January 16, 1992.
[21] *USA Today*, March 11, 1993.

sure we could "keep and bear." It's *their* wisdom that requires a threatened homeowner to wait a specified number of days before she might effectively protect herself and her family. It is *they* who endorse unreasonable invasions of privacy into the lives of freedom-loving Americans.

They are the ones who determined that a shotgun muzzle is not "legal" at 17¾ inches. And, if an FBI sniper is not going to be held accountable for the calculated killings of Vicki and Sammy Weaver, then *THEY* who made it legal are the ones who should be held accountable.

From My Cold Dead Fingers

A militia, when properly formed, are in fact the people themselves, and include all men capable of bearing arms.

—Richard Henry Lee, 1788

Only the Beginning

The abuse and usurpation of governmental power is nowhere more evident than in the legislation of more than 20,000 gun control laws in effect in this country. There has never been any constitutional, historical or common-law authorization which would allow federal, state, county or city legislatures to enact gun control laws of any kind. In fact, most individual state constitutions are even more explicit regarding the citizen's right to keep and bear arms and the government's lack of authority to impair or infringe such rights, than is our own federal Constitution's Second Amendment.

While gun control laws were being enforced over the past two-and-a-half decades, violence and crime in the U.S. have steadily skyrocketed. A failure by the government to deal promptly and severely with criminals, lenient "token" sentences handed down by liberal judges, and ineffective rehabilitation programs, have all played undeniable roles in the increase of violence in contemporary America. Criminals literally "get away with murder" in the United States of America. The average sentence given a murderer is 11 years; actual time served is less than seven. Chronic leniency in the court system has perpetuated crime and increased the numbers of repeat offenders.

From My Cold Dead Fingers

The government uses statistics on crime and violence as an excuse to confiscate guns from law-abiding citizens on grounds that "we must stop all the killing." If gun control really worked, the sponsors of such legislation should be able to show impressive corresponding reductions in crime rates. The two U.S. cities with the most stringent gun control laws—New York and Washington, D.C.—are prime examples of the complete failure of gun legislation having an impact on crime or violence.

In bold defiance of common sense, logic and the U.S. Constitution, Congress passed the Brady Bill, and President Clinton signed it into law November 30, 1993. Clinton and other powers that be in Washington—Senator Metzenbaum, Congressman Schumer, and Handgun Control, Inc., Chairwoman Sarah Brady—all promised this was "only the beginning."

The beginning of *what*? Twenty thousand failed gun control laws would suggest we're talking about the "beginning" of something else—perhaps complete disarmament. Cecil Talboy, a concerned citizen of Arizona, writes effectively: "The present federal administration and many state and local governments have become bold and impatient in their clamor for more stringent increments of control leading to complete disarmament of 'the people,' and reduction of (their) status to that of SUBJECTS." Talboy refers to "disarmament" as a "prerequisite to tyranny," and offers the premise that a direct legal approach (repeal of the Second Amendment) might arouse the general population from its state of apathy. Therefore, the more subversive method of imposing progressively harsher restrictions has been employed. Talboy reminds us Adolph Hitler once said, "We are freeing men from the responsibilities of freedom, which only a few men can bear."

On March 1, 1994, Senator Howard Metzenbaum introduced Brady Bill II. There are three more planned to follow. This series of Brady Bills—each one tougher than its predecessor—is part of a designed agenda aimed at disarming America. Gun control advocates and opponents agree the passage of the Brady Bill *is* only the beginning.

Proponents of unconstitutional government behavior have a way of throwing up smoke screens to direct the focus of the media and general citizenry where they want it. In this case, the Brady Bill was touted as a five-day waiting period during which time all U.S. citizens wishing to exercise their Second Amendment rights by purchasing a handgun must undergo a criminal background check. (Rifles and shotguns were exempt at that time, but the government's Fabian agenda has now caught up to rifles and shotguns as well.)

However, the Brady Bill goes much farther than imposing a five-day waiting period. It requires state, county and city law enforcement agencies to conduct background checks, using their own resources, manpower and budgets to enforce a *federal* mandate. The law creates a new title—a *CLEO*, or Chief Law Enforcement Officer. All CLEOs (sheriffs and police chiefs) nationwide are required to perform the background checks for all citizens living within their particular jurisdictions. Further, CLEOs are required to do background checks on citizens who travel outside their local jurisdictions and attempt to buy handguns at gun shops located within other CLEOs' jurisdictions.

The Brady Bill states that the CLEO *"... shall make a reasonable effort to ascertain within 5 business days whether receipt or possession [by the purchaser] would be in violation of the law."* CLEOs must determine if *"... a transaction would violate Federal, State or local law."* However, there's no mention as to what criteria the CLEO should use to reach that determination.

The Bureau of Alcohol, Tobacco and Firearms informed all CLEOs that the "… ATF is the Federal agency responsible for implementing the act."[22] It becomes prudent at this time to reiterate that sheriffs and chiefs of police across this country do not work for, nor do they answer to, the ATF! Also, neither the Brady Bill nor the ATF interpretation of it defines what constitutes a "reasonable effort" by the CLEO. The bill only states the CLEO *shall* make one. Contradictorily, ATF says the CLEO "… ultimately is in the best position to determine what is reasonable."[23] The kicker here is that if a CLEO fails to comply with these vague and ridiculous bureaucratic requirements, then he or she "… *shall be fined not more than $1,000, imprisoned for not more than one year, or both.*"[24]

So what we have now is a "law" that requires a county sheriff or city chief of police to abandon his or her own statutory obligations, to comply with a *federal* mandate in making a "reasonable effort" to do background checks, to make them responsible for determining the reasonableness in obeying the law, and then to throw them in jail when they don't do it right! Sounds perfectly reasonable coming from a federal government that can justify the murder of Vicki Weaver, and even babies within a religious compound at Waco, Texas (the whole story in a later chapter).

---

[22] BATF Open Letter to All Law Enforcement Agencies, January 21, 1994, p. 2.

[23] BATF Open Letter, p. 10.

[24] Brady Handgun Control Act, Section §924(a), paragraph 5.

Several sheriffs across the U.S. filed separate lawsuits challenging the constitutionality of the Brady Bill. Within days the Justice Department issued a "legal opinion" stating the federal government would not prosecute law enforcement authorities for failure to comply with Brady Bill requirements. This sudden waffling on a previously acclaimed accomplishment tends to lay a shadow of uncertainty over the whole bowl of jelly.

There are three important aspects of the "legal opinion" to keep sharply in mind: (1) This "legal opinion" would never have been issued had it not been for the lawsuits filed by sheriffs against the bill; (2) the language in the Brady Bill specifying the penalties to be assessed against a non-complying CLEO has not been removed or amended; (3) a "legal opinion" is no different from any other opinion—yours, a neighbor's, or the barber's on Main Street—because it's always subject to change and it's not legally binding.

The Justice Department's "legal opinion" states clearly the federal government lacks authority to prosecute local law enforcement officials for failing to conduct background checks. How, then, does the federal government have the authority to enact a law that by their own admission they have not the authority to enforce?

Additionally, the Brady Bill states that if a potential handgun purchaser is declared ineligible to receive a handgun, then the CLEO "... *shall provide such reasons to the individual in writing within 20 business days after receipt of the request.*"[25]

---

[25] Brady Handgun Control Act, paragraph 6(c).

On the other hand, the ATF interpretation says if the "buyer wants to contest his/her status, you (the CLEO) can be in the position of shifting the burden of tracking down absolute proof to the buyer."[26] This not only contradicts the entire presumption of innocence upon which the American judicial system is based, but it even violates the Feds' own Brady "law."

Why is the ATF interpretation so removed from the actual wording of the Brady Bill? Why is it even further from constitutional principles? Was it similar high-handed steamrolling by the same federal agency that led to a chronic (and fatal) mishandling of Branch Davidians at Waco, Texas? Did an attitude of pious impunity contribute to the sniper killings of a mother and son at Ruby Ridge, Idaho? Those arguments run a close parallel with ATF instructions to CLEOs that if a potential handgun buyer is a "fugitive, or someone you already have under investigation, you may set up surveillance and arrest the buyer when he/she returns to pick up the handgun. ... These options, and variations of these options, are *virtually limitless* ... "[27] (emphasis added).

Is the BATF out of control? If these bureaucratic interpretations, options, variations and "legal opinions" are, indeed, "virtually limitless" (and laws like the Brady Bill allow them to be), then is it really surprising that federal officials could raise the flag of victory over the charred bodies of children at Waco, and summarily justify the slayings of Randy Weaver's wife and young son?

"... we are freeing men from the responsibilities of freedom, which only a few men can bear." (Der Führer Adolph Hitler).

---

[26] BATF Open Letter, p. 11.
[27] BATF Open Letter, p. 10, paragraph 5.

"We can't be so fixated on our desire to preserve the rights of ordinary Americans .... that we are unable to think about reality." (Der President Bill Clinton).

"Ordinary Americans" had better begin asking themselves a very important question: *Am I willing to stand up and fight for my rights?* We're talking about the kind of fight waged by American colonists in the face of oppressive government tyranny. Remember the promises of Clinton, Schumer, Metzenbaum and Sarah Brady—this is *"... only the beginning."*

infringe: to act contrary to or to violate a law, obligation, or right; transgress; (obsolete:) to break down; to frustrate, to go beyond the proper or usual limits; trespass; encroach.

—A word, the meaning of which
most politicians have never learned

Unauthorized Authority

The U.S. Congress has no authority to pass gun control legislation. The framers of the Constitution made very clear the limited powers of the federal law-making body.

Section 8 of the U.S. Constitution is explicit about the powers granted the federal congress, and Section 8 is the *only* part of the document granting specific powers to the body. All the rest of it—including the Bill of Rights—deals with how its members are elected, establishes their pecking order, instructs them on how to behave, and (for what it's worth) restricts them in many things they *cannot* do. Every freedom-loving American should know exactly what the nation's federal lawmakers *are* empowered to do.

Article 1, Section 8, states simply and unequivocally:

Section 8. The Congress shall have Power

To lay and collect Taxes, Duties, Imposts and Excises, to pay the Debts and provide for the common Defence and general Welfare of the United States; but all Duties, Imposts and Excises shall be uniform throughout the United States;

To borrow Money on the credit of the United States;

To regulate Commerce with foreign Nations, and among the several States, and with Indian Tribes;

To establish an uniform Rule of Naturalization, and uniform Laws on the subject of Bankruptcies throughout the United States;

To coin Money, regulate the Value thereof, and of foreign Coin, and fix the Standard of Weights and Measures;

To provide for the Punishment of counterfeiting the Securities and current Coin of the United States;

To establish Post Offices and post Roads;

To promote the Progress of Science and useful Arts, by securing for limited Times to Authors and Inventors the exclusive Right to their respective Writings and Discoveries;

To constitute Tribunals inferior to the supreme Court;

To define and punish Piracies and Felonies committed on the high seas, and Offences against the Law of Nations;

To declare war, grant Letters of Marque and Reprisal, and make Rules concerning Captures on Land and Water;

To raise and support Armies, but no Appropriation of Money to that Use shall be for a longer Term than two Years;

To provide and maintain a Navy;

To make Rules for the Government and Regulation of the Land and naval Forces;

To provide for calling forth the Militia to execute the Laws of the Union, suppress Insurrections and repel Invasions;

To provide for organizing, arming, and disciplining, the Militia, and for governing such Part of them as may be employed in the Service of the United States, reserving to the States respectively, the Appointment of the Officers, and the Authority of training the Militia according to the discipline prescribed by Congress;

To exercise exclusive Legislation in all Cases whatsoever, over such District (not exceeding ten miles square) as may, by Cession of particular States, and the Acceptance of Congress, become the Seat of the Government of the United States, and to exercise like Authority over all Places purchased by the Consent of the Legislature of the State in which Same shall be, for the Erection of Forts, Magazines, Arsenals, dock-Yards, and other needful Buildings;—And

To make all laws which be necessary and proper for carrying into Execution the foregoing Powers, and all other Powers vested by this Constitution in the Government of the United States, or in any Department or Officer thereof.

Excuse me, but did you see anything in there about an empowerment to regulate firearms? Section 8 covers everything from taxes to credit to commerce, from currency and counterfeiting to copyrights, patents and courts systems, from piracy on the high seas and the U.S. mail to armies and navies and war declarations—even the location of Washington, D.C. But there's not a single word about gun control, and the omission was not accidental. *These* are all the powers federal lawmakers are supposed to have. And the Founding Fathers were still worried enough about them to further clarify their intentions via the Bill of Rights.

"... *the right of the people to keep and bear Arms, shall not be infringed.*"

Why, then, are there more than 20,000 restrictive gun laws on the books today?

"... *shall not be infringed.*"

Why are law-abiding Americans faced each year with at least 10,000 additional proposed restrictions? One bill proposed in 1993 would have effectively shut down hunting in an area the size of Connecticut, Delaware and Rhode Island combined. Other bills are aimed each year at prohibiting importation, manufacture, purchase, sale, transfer, receipt or transportation of handguns; at restricting or banning hundreds of models of rifles and shotguns (often based solely on appearance); at taxing gun sellers out of business, and gun buyers out of the notion, by imposing punitive license fees on legitimate dealers, exorbitant "sin" taxes on ammunition, and outrageous "user fees" on gun purchasers for such "uses" as paying the hospital bills for wounded criminals.

"... infringed."

From 1993 to early 1999, a number of omnibus gun control measures were either proposed, passed or left pending. The Violent Crime Control and Law Enforcement Act of 1993 was drawn to amend the Omnibus Crime Control and Safe Streets Act of 1968. It was intended to "increase police presence, to expand and improve cooperative efforts between law enforcement agencies and members of the community to address crime and disorder problems, and otherwise to enhance public safety ... ."

On the surface, that all sounds pretty desirable. Parts of the bill deal with murder being committed in the course of alien smuggling, terrorism in the form of violence against maritime navigation of fixed platforms, missing and exploited children, a Senate comment on out-of-wedlock births, and juvenile anti-drug and anti-gang grants in federally assisted low-income housing. That sounds good, too. Effective methods of dealing with most of the above are appropriate concerns of the U.S. Congress because the issues involve international terrorism, protecting our borders, and federal aid programs. So why does this law devote a vast majority of its pages to firearms restraining orders, firearms licensure and registration to require a photograph and fingerprints, action on firearms license application, inspection of firearms licensees' inventories and records, reports of theft or loss of

firearms, notification of names and addresses of firearms licensees, enhanced penalties for the use of a semi-automatic firearm
during commission of a crime, and a dozen more provisions
directly related to firearms regulation?[28]

Why does the issue of crime automatically become an
issue of firearms in the minds of federal lawmakers? Is a person
any less dead who is murdered with an ice pick, bare hands or a
fluffy pillow? Acts of violence perpetrated against human beings
should be treated, tried and sentenced uniformly, regardless of
whether the perpetrator used a gun, a knife, a rock or an automobile to commit the act. Each of the weapons carries an equal
potential for causing serious injury or death. Restricting and banning firearms does not reduce violence or crime. Waiting periods
are a joke. Licensing and registration are only methods of listing
law-abiding gun owners for important referencing when the time
comes to confiscate all firearms from the American populace.

Other bills born of 1993 included the Public Health and
Safety Act, which sought to "prohibit the manufacture, importation, exportation, sale, purchase, transfer, receipt, possession, or
transportation of handguns and handgun ammunition, with certain exceptions."[29]

" ... the right of the people to keep and bear Arms, shall
not be infringed."

Early 1994 brought the Gun Violence Health Care Costs
Prevention Act, to amend the Internal Revenue Code of 1986
to "increase the tax on handguns and assault weapons and to
impose a tax on the transfer of handguns and assault weapons,

---

[28] H.R.3355, In the Senate of the United States, November 19 (legislative day, November 2), 1993.
[29] S.892, In the Senate of the United States, May 5 (legislative day,
April 19), 1993.

to increase the license application fee for gun dealers, and to use the proceeds from those increases to pay medical care for gunshot victims."[30] And still another example of dogmatic brilliance surfaced in the creation of the Safe Public Housing Act, aimed at amending the United States Housing Act of 1937 to "provide for referenda among residents of public housing developments whether firearms shall be prohibited or limited in such developments, and for other purposes."[31] This jewel is designed specifically to remove guns from the hands of law-abiding citizens in inner city housing projects where drug crime and domestic violence are rampant, leaving them completely without protection and at the mercy of *armed* criminals.

Like a long line of mindless sheep clearing an imaginary barrier, they keep coming one after the other. Any explanation for the onslaught of gun control bills other than a concerted effort to disarm a nation is part of a thickening smoke screen. Yes, we discussed Knee Jerk Syndrome earlier as a reason for impassioned shallow logic, but even KJS seems to apply only to guns. A more honest analysis becomes apparent when you look at violent crimes committed with *other* weapons. After the grisly crimes of Jeffrey Dahmer, did Congress seek to regulate circular saws? After the highly publicized murders of Nicole Simpson and Ron Goldman, did anyone suggest a waiting period on serrated knives? And if we're going to attach punitive taxes to guns and ammunition to offset the high cost of treating gunshot victims, then should we not apply the same tax to high-cholesterol

---

[30] S.1798, In the Senate of the United States, January 25,1994.
[31] H.R.4062, In the House of Representatives, March 16,1994.

foods for the treatment of coronary bypass patients? Perhaps a "sin" tax on macaroni and cheese is in order. After all, heart disease kills and cripples more people than automobiles, airplanes and firearms all combined. Shall we require license fees and regulation of restaurants and grocery stores so exorbitantly high that only the most wealthy chains can afford to stay in business?

Sarah Brady climbed up on a convenient soap box after the handgun attack by John Hinckley, Jr., on President Reagan left her own husband—James Brady—partially disabled. It was a tragic incident with a devastating outcome for the Bradys. Sarah Brady now has a "cause"—to eliminate the existence of handguns in America. Unfortunately, all the Samaritan ideology in the world is not going to prevent deranged individuals like Hinckley from doing what he did, nor will it discourage sweating addicts, desperate thieves, impassioned killers, jealous husbands and wives or anybody else from doing what they do.

The five-day waiting period, as mandated in the Brady Bill (named for James Brady), is a hollow point (no pun intended). Sarah Brady and Handgun Control, Inc., fought hard for this piece of "landmark" gun control legislation, even though John Hinckley had purchased the guns used to shoot Reagan and Brady more than *five months* before the attack. Further, had the Brady Law been in effect then, and a background check conducted, Hinckley would still have gotten his weapons because he had no felony record and no public record of mental health problems at the time. In effect, what the Brady Bill really provides is one more layer of bureaucratic control applied to the constitutional rights of law-abiding American citizens ... and it's another step up for anti-gunners who will continue to try to disarm all the people of the nation.

"... shall not be infringed."

73

Handgun Control, Inc. (HCI), inspired to new heights of visionary hypothesis by passage of the Brady Bill, is pressing on with waves of oppressive anti-gun schemes. The group has powerful allies in strategic places in the Washington law-making process. Together, the lobbyists and legislators have unveiled a massive new proposal that would place monstrous powers in the hands of federal bureaucrats. This package includes a broad anti-gun movement sponsored by New York Senator Charles Schumer. The concept is to levy enormous fees, taxes and liability insurance requirements on all lawful firearms ownership, to require new licensing and registration schemes (enabling easier gun confiscation in the future), to implement gun ownership *rationing*, to impose such restrictions on licensed dealers so as to put them out of business (another whack at free enterprise), to institute bans on handguns, long guns and ammunition, and to require fingerprinting, photographing and permanent waiting periods on handgun ownership (all designed to make confiscation quick and simple in the future).

Under this proposal, a photo-identification handgun license would be required for *anyone* to buy, receive, or otherwise transfer *any* handgun or handgun ammunition. The license would only be good for two years, renewable (maybe) at some undetermined cost. The buyer must submit to fingerprinting, pass a government-mandated safety course, carry costly liability insurance, and observe a *permanent* "7-day cooling off period" prior to the completion of each and every handgun purchase.[32] (And, of course, all criminals, drug dealers and gang members will obedi-

---

[32] H.R.4300, In the House of Representatives (Schumer), and S.2053, In the Senate of the U.S., April 26 (legislative day, April 11), 1994.

ently line up for all this so the law *will* reduce crime and make the streets of America safer.)

What legitimate gun owners refer to as "gun collections" become "personal gun arsenals" under this proposed legislation. Possession of 20 firearms or 1,000 rounds of ammunition would force law-abiding citizens and sport-shooting enthusiasts (who commonly expend thousands of rounds a day at municipal shooting ranges) to submit to intensive fingerprinting and background checks by the federal government (another database for future confiscation of all legally owned guns). A collection of 1880s Peacemaker .45s (or any other type of firearm) would require a special costly "arsenal license" and tax, and would allow federal agents to conduct *on-site security inspections!*[33] This HCI/Schumer plan has the potential of impairing yet another constitutional safeguard by quietly *legalizing* "unreasonable searches and seizures."[34] (And, of course, street gangs, terrorists, black market vendors and lurking psychopaths are all anxiously awaiting their opportunities to apply for licenses and get fingerprinted so they can become legal!)

House Bill 4300 and Senate version 2053 apply so-called "gunrunning" restrictions to *everyone*—a scheme to ration all guns by limiting private and dealer transactions to one per month. (This will surely limit the number of weapons in the hands of street criminals because they can only buy one per month from any source—including the *black market!* The criminals must be devastated by this! Surely, they'll organize their own lobby to try and stop it!)

---

[33] H.R.4300 and S.2053.

[34] U.S. Constitution, Bill of Rights, Fourth Amendment.

The HCI/Schumer plan would increase the federal tax on handguns by 200 percent, and raise the tax on ammunition by nearly 500 percent. In an obvious effort to eliminate legal federal firearms licensees, the Federal Firearms License (FFL) fee would jump to $1,000 per year, closing the doors of many legitimate licensed dealers. (Black market dealers are thankful for HCI and Charles Schumer.) This sweeping legislation would prohibit "machine guns," semi-automatic military *look-alike* models, short-barreled handguns and "non-sporting" ammunition—although no definitions for the latter are provided.[35]

"... *the right to keep and bear Arms, shall not be infringed.*"

Criminals and maniacal offenders don't give a damn about any of this; they will still have easy and immediate access to their weapons of choice. Only honest dealers, dedicated collectors and sportsmen, households with a constitutional right to self-protection, and the law-abiding American mainstream, will be impacted by continued, progressively more restrictive gun control. No attempt to reduce crime, accidents or violence by government regulation of firearms has ever worked—*ever!*—and none ever will. You cannot cure a social disease by impinging on the constitutional freedoms of a society. The right to keep and bear arms did not cause social deterioration to occur in our country. A great many failed federal programs have contributed, as has the crumbling of education and economic systems, but guns didn't do it. Unemployment, an impotent justice system, rampant addiction and disease, the siphoning of billions of taxpayer dollars through a sieve called "foreign aid," a prison system impaired by corruption and overcrowding, government entitlements encour-

---

[35] H.R.4300 and S.2053.

aging welfare, homelessness, promiscuity and the general break-down of family values have all been factors, but guns have not.

The Senate version of the HCI plan opens with the typical several paragraphs of superficial justification known as "Findings and Declarations." The first claim is that "crimes committed with firearms threaten the peace and tranquility of the United States and threaten the security and general welfare of the Nation and its people."[36] Only a fool would argue that crimes committed with shovels, tire irons and knives don't do the same thing. It would be refreshing (and encouraging) to see a piece of legislation come out of Washington focusing on constitutional principles instead of today's political correctness. All their good ideas and "benevolent" purposes have no business being debated, much less enacted, if they are not constitutionally authorized. Why should one killer be treated more severely for shooting his victim in the heart than another for slashing his victim's jugular with a shard of glass? Each crime is heinous and messy—and the victims are very dead. The killer is a killer; the choice of weapon should make no difference.

Another vehicle of gun regulation introduced by then-Congressman Schumer opened with "crime, particularly crime involving guns, is a pervasive, nationwide problem."[37] Why did Mr. Schumer specifically target "guns?" Why didn't he say, "... particularly crime involving *gangs*," or "... crime involving *addicts*," or "... crime involving *angry spouses*," or "... crime involving *disgruntled postal employees*?" The *crime* is the crime; the *criminal* is the criminal. The choice of weapon is not the problem—*government* is the problem!

---

[36] S.2053.
[37] H.R.3932, In the House of Representatives, March 1, 1994.

If legislators and politicians in this country refuse to abide by state and federal constitutions, then how can they ask us to adhere to the statutes that they promulgate under the color of constitutional authority?

When all government ... shall be drawn to Washington as the center of all power, it will render powerless the checks provided ... and will become as venal and oppressive as the government from which we separated.

—Thomas Jefferson, August 1821

From My Cold Dead Fingers

The only real assault weapons are some elected officials and members of the media.

—Alan Gottlieb

Assault on the "Assaults"

"Assault weapon" is a misnomer.

Any weapon used to commit an assault is an assault weapon. That's why violence committed with bare hands is often referred to—even *legally*—as "aggravated *assault*" or "*assault* and battery." Is it not an assault if a thug shoots a convenience store clerk with a .22-caliber single-action revolver? Must a crime gun have a bayonet lug affixed to its muzzle or a banana clip protruding from its belly to fit into the "assault" category? What makes military look-alike models any more dangerous than "Old West" look-alike models? They all fire individual bullets inspired by single fingers depressing separate triggers—one at a time. Each one has the potential for traumatizing human flesh, causing severe injury or death—exactly the purpose intended during an act of self-defense. Each one has a particular value to collectors and sportsmen and shooting club enthusiasts. Each one is an addition to the arsenal of freemen's weapons that will discourage the advent of governmental dominance such as was fought and feared by the Founding Fathers.

The national media and Hollywood's penchant for pyrotechnical motion pictures have *created* the all-terrifying "assault weapon." On little or less basis than that, some anti-gunners claim assault weapons are the "weapons of choice" for criminals, and that a record number of police officers are being murdered by assault weapons. Neither claim is true.

The Florida Assault Weapons Commission compiled a report in 1990, finding that assault weapons were used in only 17 of 7,500 gun crimes in the years 1986-89. That's not 17 percent—it's just *17 crimes!* The director of the Washington, D.C., Police Firearms Section revealed in 1989 that not a single semi-automatic rifle lay among more than 3,000 weapons confiscated by police in 1988. Further, police-officer deaths in the line of duty were reported in late 1993 at the lowest level since 1968, and only about four percent of those were committed with anything resembling an assault weapon. The FBI's Uniform Crime Reporting Program says there has never been—*never bee*n—a police officer killed by a drug dealer with an Uzi.[38]

So-called assault weapons do not make good crime guns. Street criminals prefer guns they can hide. Therefore, rifles of all types—including semi-automatics with bayonet lugs and banana clips—contribute to a minimal number of crimes. The Washington, D.C., Metropolitan Police Department says less than a tenth of one percent of armed robberies in the district are committed by thieves using rifles, and only about four percent of all homicides nationwide can be attributed to killers with rifles.

There is the occasional incident of monstrous tragedy that will crystallize opinion with generous portions of negative publicity. Such is the story of Patrick Purdy. It happened in January of 1991 at a schoolyard in Stockton, California. Purdy fired 105 shots in about four minutes from a Kalashnikov-type semi-automatic rifle. His intended victims were Cambodian immigrant

---

[38] *Policy Review*, "The Violence of Gun Control," David B. Kopel, Winter 1993.

school children. Thirty-five were wounded, and six of them sub-sequently died.

The press had a field day. Stories of incredible tragedy and suffering draw reporters the way roadkill attracts maggots. And in their haste to be first and the most sensational, errors are common and much damage is done. Inaccurate reports by the national media portrayed Purdy with an *automatic* AK-47, and said such weapons could be bought over the counter. Such a frenzy ensued about the weapon he used that little was revealed about the killer. After all, he was dead, anyway, having killed himself with a pistol at the end of his shooting frenzy.

The man was sick and dangerous. He'd been arrested many times—first at age 14. His rap sheet included incidents of robbery and assault, dealing in stolen property, criminal con-spiracy, assaulting a police officer and weapons violations. His felony crimes had been reduced to misdemeanors. Two dozen arrests had never left him behind bars more than a few weeks at a time. Before the shooting rampage at a schoolyard filled with children, he told a California mental health worker he was con-sidering a mass murder. A parole report called him "a danger to himself and others."

So why was Patrick Purdy on the street? Why was no one ever held accountable for allowing him the freedom to commit murder at a schoolyard? Because no one could see beyond the horrible visual image painted by the media of a madman with a machine gun mowing down helpless children at school. The social and political focus, then, was on the weapon—*not the madman!*

But it didn't happen that way. He did not have an auto-matic AK-47. He did not spray the schoolyard with a machine gun (which, incidentally, would have spent *thousands* of rounds in four minutes). Anyone with a lever- or bolt-action hunting rifle could have duplicated Purdy's rate of fire. The only thing sensational about this terrible incident was a madman shooting children. The media all but exonerated the killer by depicting the weapon—and the wrong weapon, at that!—as the villain.

Semi-automatic "assault" weapons like the one used by Purdy differ from popular models of deer-hunting rifles only in appearance. Lawmakers trying to regulate them have had a tough nut to crack just defining them. Their efforts usually lead to a list of features like bayonet lugs, curved magazines or plastic stocks. Some lawmakers (Senators Dennis DeConcini and Joseph Biden) have had such difficulty defining assault weapons that they've used a ban-by-name approach, having to list each gun by name that's targeted by their proposed legislation. DeConcini listed 17 specific guns by name in his Anti-Drug Assault Weapons Limitation Act of 1989. California passed a law naming approximately 60 illegal "assault" weapons by model name. Maryland enacted a waiting period on two dozen named models.

And while the debate rages on over defining what they are, which ones are, what their characteristics are, or how they may differ from other models, their lack of popularity with criminals continues to remain obvious. Of 305 murders committed in Baltimore in 1990, only seven involved rifles of any kind, and even fewer were semi-automatic rifles or shotguns.[39] In Bexar County, Texas, including the city of San Antonio, "assault" weapons were used in only 0.2 percent of homicides from 1987 to 1992.[40] A gun-by-gun count of confiscated weapons by Denver

---

[39] *Baltimore Evening Sun*, February 11, 1991.

[40] "Assault Weapons as a Public Health Hazard," Kalousdian and Loeb, *Journal of the American Medical Association*, vol. 268, 1992.

police in March of 1991 turned up only 14 "assault" weapons out of 1,752 total.[41] Of more than 4,000 guns seized by Los Angeles police in 1988, only three percent could be included in a sweeping definition of "assault weapon."[42] In Florida, so-called assault weapons were used in only 17 of 7,500 gun crimes between the years 1986-89.[43] New Jersey could not find a single murder case involving a *rifle*, much less a semi-automatic rifle.[44] Only 80 "assault-type" rifles were found among *16,000* guns seized by New York police in 1988.[45]

The plain truth here is: *The criminals are not using what the anti-gun lobby and politicians are calling the criminals' "weapons of choice"!*

Anti-gunners supporting prohibition of "assault weapons" have resorted to the results of national polls to justify their ambitions. However, they are conducting their research with bias and ignorance. A Gallup poll taken a few weeks after Patrick Purdy's massacre at the Stockton schoolyard showed that 72 percent of those asked favored outlawing "assault weapons." But the pollsters did not reveal that an AK-47 had erroneously been tied to the killings, or that the same damage could have been done with a lever-action .30-30 carbine. A 1989 NBC/Wall Street Journal poll showed 74 percent of Americans in favor of banning the sale

---

[41] *Southtown Economist*, June 12, 1990.

[42] Detective Jimmy L. Trahin of L.A.P.D. Firearms/Forensics Ballistics Unit testifying for U.S. Senate Report, 1989.

[43] "Assault Weapons Crime Survey in Florida...," 1990.

[44] *Newark Star-Ledger*, July 18, 1989.

[45] Associated Press Report, *White Plains Reporter-Dispatch*, March 27, 1989

of "assault rifles in the United States."[46] Ironically, Congress has already banned manufacture of genuine assault rifles (automatics) in 1986.

Handgun Control, Inc., has used advantageously a Texas poll that shows 89 percent of Texans favoring a "mandatory seven-day waiting period to purchase a high-caliber, fast-firing assault rifle."[47] Since 1934, there has been a *six-month transfer application period* for the "high-caliber, fast-firing" machine-gun-type weapons described in the poll.[48] Respondents in the poll were asked a leading question, and their overall response has been used by HCI as an argument to ban firearms as common as Remington 7400 hunting rifles, Browning DA shotguns, Colt .32 pistols (a small model chosen for self-protection by women who would carry it in a purse or handbag), and Crossman BB guns!

While some journalists may fumble around in ignorance, inadvertently misstating facts or misnaming firearms, others have admittedly left the trail of objective reporting. In 1989, *Time* magazine did a feature entitled, "Street Favorites: Assault Weapons Available Over the Counter." There are two fallacies within this very title. First, the so-called "assault weapons" are not "street favorites," and are not even *preferred* by street criminals or gangs. Second, at the risk of becoming redundant, assault weapons are *not* available over the counter.

"Assault weapons" is a terminology so corrupted by gun prohibition advocates and the media that it's difficult to distin-

---

[46] "The 'Assault Weapon' Panic," Morgan and Kopel, Independence Institute, Golden, CO, April 10, 1993, p. 37.

[47] The Texas Poll, Hartke-Hanks Communications, August 4-19, 1990.

[48] The Texas Poll, August 4-19, 1990.

guish between the six o'clock news and the latest Schwarzeneger movie. The *Time* story went on to name the AK-47 as one of those "street favorites ... available over the counter," and described the weapon as "Soviet designed, adopted by armed forces in many nations." (This is *Time* magazine, a periodical many Americans have come to rely on as credible.) In truth, the AK-47 is *not* available over the counter, and is regulated with the same stringent controls as applied to full machine guns since 1934. And if, perchance, *Time* thought it was talking about the semi-automatic AKS (which looks like its more volatile cousin), it should be noted that model is not Soviet-designed and has never been adopted by the armed forces of *any* nation.[49]

Further, KABC-TV and KABC radio in Los Angeles have waged their own lopsided campaign to distort the truth and influence popular opinion. Bill Peters, a news correspondent there, testified before the U.S. Senate that the "battle is too critical," and that he considered it his "responsibility" to "inform the public of the dangers to society posed by military assault rifles and to help build support for getting rid of them." Peters explained his stations' strategy of emphasizing news stories of crimes committed with semi-automatic rifles in Los Angeles while playing down or omitting stories of crimes involving conventional revolvers. KABC even rigged a news segment showing 9mm handguns as being capable of very rapid firing coupled with unusual accuracy, by splicing together two different tape segments.[50]

---

[49] "The 'Assault Weapon' Panic," Morgan and Kopel, Independence Institute, Golden, CO, April 10, 1993, p. 39.

[50] "The 'Assault Weapon' Panic," Morgan and Kopel, p. 82.

Journalists will often defend their actions—most *any* actions—with an enigmatic assertion that the "public has the right to know." It's almost as if they achieve moralistic impunity by *blaming* the public for their own indiscretions while stonewalling the basic ideal that the public, indeed, has the right to know *the truth!*

Confusing the public has become a far more consistent media pastime than imparting the truth, and it's not at all by accident. Liberal politics within the national media are as commonplace today as exaggerated doses of political correctness. Recognizing the strong link between left-wing ideology and mainstream journalism, Josh Sugarmann—head of the anti-gunner group Violence Policy Center—used this natural marriage to advance his own agenda. After noting in 1988 that the handgun-ban issue was no longer making headlines on the evening news, Sugarmann wrote a "strategy memo" for the gun prohibition movement, explaining simply (and honestly) that the menacing appearance of semi-automatic weapons, and the public's confusion over fully automatic machine guns versus semi-automatic assault weapons, could only increase public support for restrictions on these firearms.[51]

Sugarmann was right. His distinction as one of the most technically knowledgeable people in the anti-gun movement brought immediate attention from the media. Some powerful Washington lawmakers—Senators Hatch, Thurmond, Simpson and others—used the ploy to muster support for banning these guns, writing in a Senate report: "... they have been referred to as 'assault weapons,' a term which conjures up some idea of ter-

---

[51] "Assault Weapons and Accessories in America," Josh Sugarmann, 1988.

rible weapons that have no purpose other than killing innocent people."[52]

They all know they are perpetuating a lie. Bill Peters knows it or he would not orchestrate his newscasts to highlight stories supporting only his point of view. Josh Sugarmann knows it or there would be no need for a "strategy" to influence public opinion. The Washington senators certainly know it or they would not have deliberately conspired to paint a horrifying picture of innocent victims riddled with bullets from weapons incorrectly (and knowingly) labeled as "assault weapons." The wildest misstatements have come from anti-gunner groups like Handgun Control, Inc., continuing to assert that "assault weapons" are the "weapons of choice" of gangs and criminals, and, further, that these firearms (different from most only in appearance) are "weapons of war."

Are these false claims only a product of HCI spokeswoman Sarah Brady's ignorance, or are they calculated to promote gun prohibition by further augmenting the lie? Perhaps it's a combination of these and other factors. At any rate, an impressionable American public is being duped by clever strategists and spinmasters. Many of those espousing the benefits of gun control and prohibition rely heavily on the First Amendment provisions for freedom of speech and of the press. They (especially the media) would fight tooth-and-nail if anyone ever threatened to take away—*infringe* upon—those rights. It's a matter of moral discretion, however, whether or not they tell the truth.

---

[52] "The 'Assault Weapon' Panic," Morgan and Kopel, p. 82.

We have held, however, that state legislatures are not subject to federal direction.

—*New York* v. *U.S.*, 505 U.S. 144 (1992)

Sensationalism and Emotionalism

Together with freedom of the press, the right to keep and bear arms became one of the rights most prized by the colonists. Those "rights"—if used properly—are protections against governmental usurpations and tyranny; if abused, they can both be deadly.

Abuse and manipulation by the media in distorting the truth about gun control has entrapped many Americans in the snare of illusion. The propaganda and sensationalism as perpetrated by the media (and the federal government) has misled many Americans into believing guns cause crime and violence. It is by this avenue that legislation, millions of dollars in resources, honest attempts at effective law enforcement, and *jillions* of tax dollars have all been misdirected and wasted on "feel good" laws that simply do not work.

The ban on "assault rifles" has been praised by anti-gunners, many proud politicians, the media, and even President Clinton, as effective legislation in "protecting our children and our police officers" from murderers. But it's a ruse—a tactic—built on the premise that if you tell someone the same lie often and consistently enough, it begins to take on a veil of truth. However, in their attempts to convince Americans they'll be safer with more gun control, they are virtually advocating the disarming of a nation without a thought given to who'll take responsibility for rampant crime and carnage and governmental oppression when private citizens no longer have the ability or means to protect themselves.

Murders, assaults and drive-by shootings are heinous and abhorrent acts of cowardice. But, again, the ugliness of the crimes and criminals is often lost in a sensationalized media focus on the *weapons* involved—if, in fact, a *gun* was used. Knee Jerk Syndrome rears its predictable head, then, in the form of emotional pleas for more gun control. Ironically, the weapons used by some of the most notorious mass murderers of the 20th century (Jeffrey Dahmer, John Wayne Gacey, Charles Manson, Ted Bundy, Richard Speck) have received little or no attention from the media or lawmakers because their "weapons of choice" were something other than guns. And yet, the victims of those killers suffered unfathomably hideous and agonizing deaths.

Conversely, the *benefits* afforded by guns in saving lives, preventing injuries and protecting private property exceed the negative statistics on firearms by at least 25 to one. An overwhelming preponderance of data shows between 25 and 75 lives may be saved by a gun for every life lost to a gun.[53] Think of the difference it would have made to seven terrified nurses in a Chicago boarding house had one of them confronted Richard Speck with a gun. (The issue of crime control by armed citizens is examined extensively in a subsequent chapter.)

The graph on the next page illustrates further the safest and most effective tool in instances of self-defense by comparing injury rates of victims.[54]

---

[53] *The Journal of the Medical Association of Georgia*, Edgar A. Suter, M.D., March 1994, p. 146.

[54] *Point Blank: Guns and Violence in America*, Gary Kleck, Aldine de Gruyter, Hawthorne, NY, 1991.   **92**

Rates of Injury
by Victim's Method of Protection

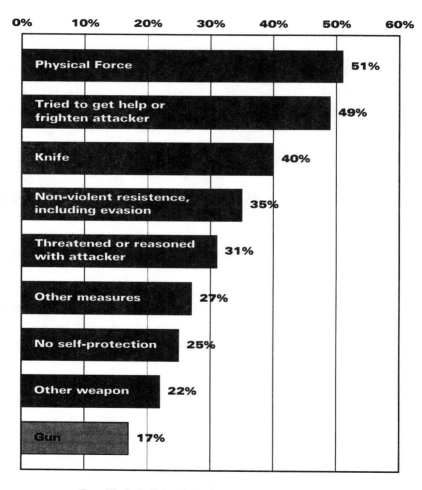

From Kleck, G. *Point Blank: Guns and Violence in America*.
Hawthorne, NY: Aldine de Gruyter. 1993. Table 4.4.

So why does government expect a law-abiding citizenry to give up its guns when statistics show that using them against would-be attackers results in a safe resolution 83 percent of the time? Bob Corbin, former president of the National Rifle Association, says government finds new ways every year to say, "You can't be trusted with your rights, so we'll 'manage' them for you." Corbin goes on to say each time that happens, more freedoms are lost ... the state grows stronger at the expense of individual liberties ... government creeps toward authoritarian rule ... and the Second Amendment becomes more precious and endangered.[55]

The media, anti-gun lobby groups and government officials continue to insist guns cause crime, violence, suicide and accidental shootings of children. The plain truth is: guns *deter* crime and violence, and "... amongst tools of suicide, guns are neither uniquely available, uniquely lethal, nor causal of suicide."[56] Further, children are far more likely to suffer accidental death by traffic accident, drowning, burning or suffocating than by gunshot.

A graph on the following page defines clearly where guns rate alongside other causes of children's accidental deaths.[57] Dead last on the list, guns are still brought to the forefront by a media mentality that thrives on sensationalism and corrupts the craft of journalism to promote a leftist agenda.

---

[55] *American Rifleman*, "The President's Column," Robert K. Corbin, June 1994, p. 61.

[56] *The Journal of the Medical Association of Georgia*, March 1994, p. 140.

[57] National Safety Council, "Accident Facts 1991," 1992.

Children's Accidental Deaths, 1991

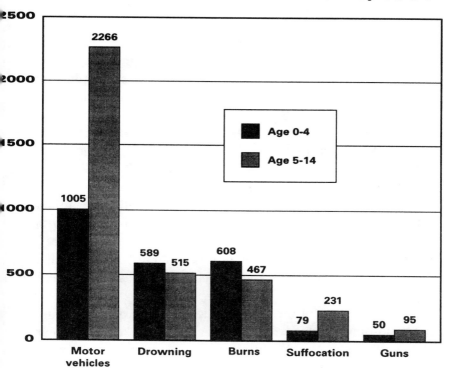

From National Safety Council. *Accident Facts 1991*. 1992.

The most basic causes of crime in America are the break-down of the family unit, the moral collapse of society, the loss of human dignity through socialistic welfare programs, poverty, the promotion of violence through entertainment and the media, the profitability of drug trafficking, substance abuse and racism. These social ills have no more to do with gun ownership than spousal abuse has to do with getting married.

In 1976, Washington, D.C., enacted stringent gun control laws, including a ban on handguns and new gun sales. In the same year, "... the homicide rate before the law was 26.9 (derived from population and homicide statistics) and then tripled to 80.6 by 1991—despite or due to the law?"[58]

Where people are unarmed and defenseless, criminals are most bold. Criminals literally go out of their way to avoid potential victims who appear to be armed. Doesn't it make sense to have the *safest* and *most effective* tool of self-defense readily available when needed? Who but the lurking, stalking criminal benefits from a waiting period? Incidents of self-defense with firearms occur daily, saving as many as *five lives per minute!*[59] Most of these cases receive little or no attention from the media, however, because there's no gore—no basis for sensationalism or emotionalism.

Perhaps one of the most publicized cases demonstrating the unquestionable need for private citizens to keep and bear arms is the Reginald Denny assault incident in Los Angeles. Denny's case *did not* involve a firearm. Yet the nation witnessed a most cruel and deliberate, vicious and cowardly act of violence.

---

[58] *The Journal of the Medical Association of Georgia*, March 1994, p. 144.

[59] *The Journal of the Medical Association of Georgia*, March 1994, p. 144.

Denny—the unsuspecting trucker who drove into a riot in progress—was nearly beaten to death. The entire ordeal could have (and *would* have) been avoided if Denny had simply raised a gun to the window of his truck.

Just as federal lawmakers seem committed to a back door approach for dealing with crime, gun control advocates have a reverse perception of the rightful place for guns in our society. To most of them, a *gun* means a *crime*; a gun is an instrument built, sold, purchased and possessed solely for the purpose of killing innocent people, and so on and so on ... In reality, the voices of leadership (lobbyists, politicians, journalists) should be championing the existence of firearms—and the right to keep and bear them—as tools of safety and security. The sensational headlines are made by an emotional media reacting to a microscopic segment of society committing ugly acts. It's the millions and millions of responsible gun owners in America who *don't* make the news.

Dr. John E. Smialek, chief medical examiner for the state of Maryland, says, "... it's not the weaponry that's become more deadly; it's the mentality."

The "mentality" Smialek refers to is the product of a societal disorder. It spawns a laissez-faire attitude about death and negates the value of human life. In view of facts as supported by statistics, surveys and the truth, an equally dangerous mentality appears to be that of the media, government officials, politicians and left-leaning anti-gunners who espouse the fallacies of gun control.

Laws that forbid the carrying of arms ... disarm only those who are neither inclined nor determined to commit crimes ... Such laws make things worse for the assaulted and better for the assailants ... .

—Thomas Jefferson, 1764

The Power of Gun Control

Police officers throughout this country are being asked (or mandated) to violate their oaths of office by legislatures that continue to stack gun control laws on top of gun control laws. Some cops have refused to do it. Others have complied, albeit reluctantly in some cases. Some have done so willingly under the assumption that all laws, good or bad, must be enforced irrespective of their constitutionality.

In the more specific area of gun control, some cops have said they do not agree with the concept, but a law is a law. A scant few of these same officers have said they would refuse to *confiscate* guns from law-abiding citizens, while others would enforce such a law if ordered to do so.

The ultimate question (regrettably not an entirely hypothetical one) has been posed to our nation's police officers. "If it were the law and you were ordered to do so, would you *shoot at innocent citizens*?" Typical responses always include a refusal and a qualifying phrase: "... but that would never happen." Unfortunately, it *has* happened, and it *will* happen again if the Federal Government continues to demand the complete disarming of the nation's citizens.

In all of history very few of the earth's inhabitants have lived in a free society. One need not look far to prove the adage that "power kills and absolute power kills absolutely." For example, the former Soviet Union, Communist China, Nazi Germany, the Khmer Rouge of Cambodia, Communist Vietnam and Communist Yugoslavia (all countries exercising absolute power) have accounted for over 122,535,000 documented cold-blooded murders. Another 8,361,000 innocent citizens have been annihilated by totalitarian governments in Communist Afghanistan, Angola, Laos, Ethiopia, North Korea, Rumania, Argentina, Burundi, Chile, Croatia, Czechoslovakia, Indonesia, Iran, Rwanda, Spain, Sudan and Uganda.[60] All this carnage occurred during the 20th century.

Germany's Adolph Hitler not only murdered millions of Jews, but carried his purification of the race on to include the elimination of Slavs, Gypsies, homosexuals, French, Balts, Czechs and others. Joseph Stalin, V.I. Lenin and some of their Soviet successors "... murdered some 61,911,000 Soviet citizens and foreigners. ... Then there is Mao Tse-tung's China, Chiang Kai-shek's China, the militarists' Japan, Yahya Khan's Pakistan, Pol Pot's Cambodia, and others who have murdered in the millions."[61]

Most of this incredible slaughter was carried out by the nations' police or armies (sometimes one and the same). Most of the victims were living under the oppressive rule of powerful, elite governments that felt comfortable with the practice of genocide. Had the right to *keep and bear arms* existed in any one of these countries, history might have been written quite differently.

---

[60] *Social Science and Modern Society*, "Megamurders," R.J. Rummel, September/October 1992, p. 48.

[61] *Social Science and Modern Society*, Sept./Oct. 1992, pp. 50-51.

All these hundreds of millions of murder victims had just two things in common: they were living where the governments had unrestricted and unchecked power, and they had no means of defending themselves with anything more lethal than garden tools and household utensils. They were subject to indiscriminate robberies and rapes, tortures, killings and involuntary servitude. As common citizens they were incapable of defending themselves because, in their countries of omnipotent governments, only the criminals and police (armies) possessed firearms.

Aaron Zelman, a Holocaust historian who founded Jews for the Preservation of Firearms Ownership (JPFO), defines the entire Holocaust as the result of disarmament. Zelman has since dedicated his life to the preservation of freedom's principles—particularly the right to keep and bear arms. He says, "There is no doubt in my mind that millions of lives could have been saved if the people were not brainwashed about gun ownership, and had been well-armed. It truly frightens me to see how the government, media, and some police groups in America are pushing for the same mind-set."[62]

Fueled with memories of the deadly Dachau Concentration Camp, Zelman addresses contemporary anti-gunners passionately: "These Sarah Brady types must be educated to understand that because we have an armed citizenry, that a dictatorship has not yet happened in America. These anti-gun fools are more dangerous to liberty than street criminals or foreign spies. You cowards—you gun haters—you don't deserve to live

---

[62] *American Survival Guide*, Aaron Zelman, November 1990, p. 65.

in America. Go live in the Soviet Union if you love gun control so damn much."[63]

Near the end of a blood-soaked century in which millions of innocent people were murdered by their own governments, the Clinton regime proposed and enacted upon the American people the so-called "Crime Bill" of 1994. This bill—a "crime" itself—should probably have been called the "Enslavement Bill." For openers, it will cost American taxpayers in excess of $30,000,000,000 (that's "b" as in *billion*) to finance the most stringent gun control ever enacted by Congress, and to provide Big Brother with even more sophisticated ways to legally seize your personal property.

And if that were not enough, Clinton's "Crime Bill" ensured that 5,000 members of the Hong Kong Royalty Police would be employed to work the streets of the United States of America. The Crime Bill reads: *"Not later than six months after the date of enactment of the Act, the Attorney General, in concert with the Director of the Federal Bureau of Investigation, the Administrator of the Drug Enforcement Agency, the Commissioner of the Immigration and Naturalization Service, and the Commissioner of the Customs Service, shall report to Congress and the President on the effort made, and the success of such efforts, to recruit and hire former Royal Hong Kong Police officers into Federal law enforcement positions. The report shall discuss any legal or administrative barriers preventing a program of adequate recruitment of former Royal Hong Kong Police officers."*[64]

---

[63] *American Survival Guide*, Nov. 1990, p. 66.

[64] S. 17091, Section §5108, "Report on Success of Royal Hong Kong Police Recruitment."

Why? Who conceived the idea to employ *foreign* police officers not bound by a constitutional oath to "protect and defend?" How will this reduce crime on the streets of America? Have we mentioned somewhere before the push to place us all under one large centralized *world* government? An important step toward that end is removing all guns from the hands of all common Americans. Before the elections of 1994, lawmakers in Washington busied themselves feverishly proposing more new gun control measures. Some of them are listed below.

S.108	Bans Many Imported Guns, Moynihan (D-NY)
S.639	Bans Many Rifles, Shotguns and Handguns, DeConcini (D-AZ)
S.653	Bans Many Rifles, Shotguns and Handguns, Metzenbaum (D-OH)
S.892	Bans All Handguns, Chafee (D-RI)
H.R.893	Bans Many Rifles, Shotguns and Handguns, Gutierrez (D-IL)
H.R.1421	Bans Many Rifles, Shotguns and Handguns, Stark (D-CA)
H.R.1472	Bans Many Rifles, Shotguns and Handguns, Schumer (D-NY)
H.R.1501	Bans All Handguns, Yates (D-IL)
H.R.1568	Bans Many Rifles, Shotguns and Handguns Gibbons (D-FL)

H.R.1706   Bans Many Rifles, Shotguns and Handguns,
Mfume (D-MD)

H.R.1734   Bans Nonsporting Handguns, Gutierrez (D-IL)

H.R.3132   Bans All Handguns, Owens (NY)

H.R.3184   Bans Many Rifles, Shotguns and Handguns,
Reynolds (D-IL)

H.R.1571   Bans Many Rifles, Shotguns and Handguns,
Hughes (D-NJ)

H.R.3932/S.1878/S.1882 Bans Guns, Ammo, Primers,
Magazines, and Dictates New York City-
style Licensing, Schumer (D-NY) and
Metzenbaum (D-OH)

H.R.4300/S.2053 Requires States to Impose New York
City-style Licensing on Handgun Owners,
Schumer (D-NY) and Bradley (D-NJ)

The United States Congress has no authority to propose
or enact a single one of these costly and destructive measures.
Refer again, if you will, to Article 1, Section 8, of the Constitution. No provision there grants the Federal Government authority
to enact a single gun control law—not to mention the 20,000-plus
gun regulations already passed and forced upon the law-abiding
American citizenry. Such a provision does not appear anyplace
else because that was never the vision or intent of the Founding
Fathers. There is no provision for a *"crime bill,"* either; that
authority was specifically reserved for the several states. The
above-named lawmakers—and others with like minds—should

not only be removed from their offices and stripped of the privilege of serving free-American constituencies, but also *arrested and tried for the crime of treason* for violating the sanctity of the principles upon which our young "free" nation was built.

Each year Congress makes new laws, raises taxes to pay for ineffective enforcement of those laws, and further increases the power and control of the Federal Government. There are three basic commodities at stake—all of which equate to power, and will determine the difference between total government oppression and a free republic of the people, depending on who possesses them. Those commodities are money, land and *guns!*

Money. The Federal Government already controls the money. It determines how much in taxes you'll pay, and how many *zillions* of those tax dollars are flung over our borders and across the oceans for symbolic, useless and wasteful "foreign aid." It controls interest rates and other aspects of the banking system, and dictates what state and local governments must do to qualify for education and infrastructure appropriations. (Remember such tactics as withholding "federal highway funds" if everybody did not drive 55 miles per hour?) Manufacturers are told how and where to produce their products, how those products must be packaged and labeled and sold to whom, and for how much profit. In just 45 years, working Americans have gone from paying about two percent of their income in federal taxes to 25 percent. There's no end in sight, and the *taxpayers* don't have a voice in the matter. Government controls the money.

Land. About 50 percent of the land area within the United States is "owned" or controlled by the Federal Government. While there never has been any constitutional authority for the federal government to own more land than needed for military bases and post offices, additional land acquisition is occurring at a rate of about 1,000 acres *per day.* Why? To control the land is to control the people. Control of the land is easily accomplished by controlling the water on the land. Congress, through a revised version of the Clean Water Act, plans to grant control of 100 percent of the water in America to the Environmental Protection Agency.[65] That, coupled with endangered species critical habitat designations, the Wild and Scenic Rivers System, the National Rivers program, undefined "wetlands" delineation, implementation of Rangeland 94 regulations, radical reform of the mining industry, the unauthorized National Biological Survey, United Nations' World Heritage sites, and more (this list could go on forever), puts total control of the land very much within reach of the Federal Government. *To control the land is to control the people!*

Guns. When every living American between the events of birth and death possesses a Social Security number ... and every citizen is assigned some other form of national identification ... and free enterprise is reduced to a system of socialized "communitarianism" ... and private property rights have been washed away by Congress-approved bureaucratic regulation ... and wage-earners can no longer earn enough to pay taxes *and* support families without relying on government "entitlements" ... and an entire nation of common people realize they are "subjects" to the autocrats on Capitol Hill ... and when the governmental foot rises for that final step into a Giant Central World Government under control of the United Nations ... what is the one thing that will keep the several states free? AMERICANS OWNING GUNS! That is why relentless efforts by Washington lawmakers to remove guns from the hands of law-abiding citi-

---

[65] S.1114-II.

zens must be regarded as a capital infringement on the rights and freedoms of a people—not to mention the security of a nation.

The behavior of Americans is becoming more and more commanded (mandated) and less and less spontaneous (free). The United States Government does not trust civilian Americans with their own rights and freedoms. Therefore, they must be registered, catalogued, regulated and watched. There's an effort afoot to plant special microchips into every telephone and computer in America so Big Brother can keep better tabs on the masses.[66] Bureaucrats claim it's needed to track terrorists, drug-runners and spies, but how do they justify such flagrant violation of the "... *right of the people to be secure in their persons, houses, papers and effects, against unreasonable searches ...?*"[67] They don't. They don't even try, because that violation is by design, not accident.

Loss of personal rights and freedoms within a populace is the natural product of a power-grabbing government. The more centralized the power, the more control by that government. The more totalitarian the government, the more frustration (and violence) in society ... and the greater the likelihood of genocide.

"In a highly centralized system, a loss on one issue may result in a loss on all, including even one's life."[68]

Quincy Wright wrote in his book *A Study of War,* "It appears that absolutist states with geographically and functionally centralized governments under autocratic leadership are likely to

---

[66] *Time* Magazine, "Who Should Keep the Keys?", Phillip Elmer-DeWitt, March 14, 1994, pp. 90-91.

[67] U.S. Constitution, Bill of Rights, Fourth Amendment.

[68] *Social Science and Modern Society,* "The Politics of Cold Blood," R.J. Rummel, November/December 1989, p. 35.

be most belligerent, while constitutional states with geographically and functionally federalized governments under democratic leadership are likely to be most peaceful."

While every murder is a tragedy, the destruction and loss of life attributed to street criminals of the 20th century is minuscule as compared to the enormity of government-sponsored murders and genocides in the world. Our greatest single fear today should be of our own federal government's insatiable affinity for usurpation of powers and increased dominance over the citizens of the several states.

These Sarah Brady types must be educated to understand that because we have an armed citizenry, a dictatorship has not yet happened in America. These anti-gun fools are more dangerous to liberty than street criminals or foreign spies.

—Aaron Zelman, founder of
Jews for the Preservation of Firearms Ownership

From My Cold Dead Fingers

Millions of people armed in the holy cause of liberty, and in such a country as that which we possess, are invincible by any force which our enemy can send against us.

—Patrick Henry

In America, Too

The history of the United States, too, has been scarred by "laws" of prejudice and hate, resulting in widespread civil rights violations and even mass murder. Before the Emancipation Proclamation and the Civil War, it was a "law" that whites should *own* blacks. Even after the black Americans were "freed," they were forced to live under laws of prejudice. By "law," they were prohibited from eating in the same restaurants as whites, from living in the same neighborhoods, from using the same hospitals or even drinking from the same public fountains.

These *"laws"* were enforced by our nation's police. (Remember, all laws must be enforced, *irrespective of their constitutionality.*)

Further, even as "freemen" of the nation, blacks were forbidden from owning guns. When angry mobs and hooded nightriders came to burn homes, commit whippings and lynchings, or to indiscriminately shoot at homes while families slept, "free" black Americans were forced to stand helpless and watch their loved ones be victimized and killed. Often their only defense was to "escape" to the refuge of servile obedience. Gun control laws then bore the same labels as they do today: "... for your own good," or "... for the good of the country."

Today, black Americans face the bondage of social welfare programs and poverty. The Reverend Jesse Jackson types and the NAACP have done more to enslave the Afro-American community than all the southern plantation owners put together.

A new freedom movement within the black community is being led by Jesse Peterson, founder of B.O.N.D. (Brotherhood Organization of a New Destiny). This "Renaissance Man" is telling blacks to quit "blaming racism for all our troubles. So-called black 'leaders' use racism as a way to build their own agendas."

(Could this mean you, Reverend?)

Peterson writes: "Jesse Jackson, Maxine Waters, Mayor Tom Bradley and all of those like them are the real enemies of black Americans. Self-control and self-respect do not have to loot or burn in order to gain recognition ... Even a fool knows that to build character one must work and sustain one's own self. We are being misled ... The greatest power the enemy has is over our minds. Through perpetuating the clever and persuasive lie that our real stumbling block is outward and white, rather than inward and black. The enemy of my race is amongst our own kind."[69]

Black-on-black crime today is pervasive—especially in the inner cities of America. It is a social ill and has nothing to do with the constitutional right to keep and bear arms. Politicians repealing the Second Amendment and banning all the guns in America is like so many cats in a litter box, scratching a thin cover over a mess but doing nothing to remove it. Jesse Peterson knows that and is working hard to cut through the layers of socio-complacency and attack the disease at its source.

---

[69] B.O.N.D. Newsletter, Jesse Peterson, July/August 1992.

Another page of American history involved an exodus west by pioneers in pursuit of land, riches and better lives. As the trailblazers, settlers and builders moved into the new territory, they found other cultures and civilizations inhabiting their Promised Land. Competition for the land became a blood-bath. American Indians were slaughtered for being in the way. General Custer and Kit Carson were glorified as western heroes. Entire villages of men, women and children were annihilated by the soldiers of a nation pressing for expansion. Native American survivors were left defenseless through governmental agreements which required Indians to give up their weapons. The government promised to protect them, and placed them on reservations. Millions had died.

Another American disgrace was the incarceration of Japanese Americans during World War II. In Gestapo fashion, the U.S. Government rounded up all Japanese in the "land of the free"—especially those living along the west coast—and put them in concentration camps until the end of the war. They had committed no crimes; there were no warrants or investigations. They were *citizens!* The Constitution was forsaken "for the good of the country."

(Does that sound familiar?)

Another despicable governmental decree came from a state governor in the face of religious freedom. It happened October 27, 1838. Missouri Governor Lilburn W. Boggs issued an order calling for the "extermination or expulsion of Mormons."[70]

A Mormon militia had been formed in Caldwell County, and was betrayed by its commander into "government" hands.

---

[70] *The 1838 Mormon War in Missouri*, Stephen C. LeSuer, University of Missouri Press, Columbia, MO, 1987, p. 262..

Major Gen. Samuel Lucas forced the Mormons to "give up their arms of every description." Later, Mormon leader Joseph Smith wrote in his journal that his followers were taken out of the city and forced to give up their arms, appalled by the taking of "their own property, which no government on earth had a right to require."[71]

As is always the case when a ruler grants himself absolute authority over his "subjects," enforcement became tyranny. Boggs' troops freely ransacked the Mormons' homes, plundered their valuables, forced the Mormons to sign over their deeds to property, and raped their women. About 80 Mormon men were taken prisoners and the rest were ordered to leave the state. Further, they were warned that if more than three of them were caught assembled together in any one place, they would be shot on sight.

Not until 138 years later—on June 25, 1976—did Governor Christopher S. Bond rescind the 1838 extermination order issued by Governor Boggs. Governor Bond said, "Whereas, Governor Boggs' order clearly contravened the rights to life, liberty, property and religious freedom as guaranteed by the Constitution of the United States ... (and) expressing on behalf of all Missourians our deep regret for the injustice and undue suffering which was caused ... ."[72]

There are those who would assert that government never learns by its past indiscretions. Johan Galtung, a well-known peace researcher alleges, "... the CIA has been carrying out very

---

[71] *The New American*, Robert W. Lee, February 1994.
[72] *The 1838 Mormon War in Missouri*, Stephen C. LeSuer, p. 262.

much the same thing as Hitler's holocaust ... and has rubbed out 6 million people throughout the world."[73]

Freedom is (and always has been) worth fighting for—even dying for. Patrick Henry said he would prefer death to life without liberty. The colonists of the several states adopted that credo and a new republic was born. Today, the enemy is less recognizable, and in the current fight for freedom and liberty, we must know and be totally aware of whom the enemy really is, both "foreign and domestic." This fight should not be over the unconstitutional control of firearms, but over the *constitutional control of government!*

---

[73] *Social Science and Modern Society,* "The Politics of Cold Blood," R.J. Rummel, November/December 1989, p. 40.

The gun debate isn't just about waiting periods, semi-automatic bans, licensing, registration, handgun bans or the Second Amendment; it's about liberty, and the fundamental beliefs that make democracy possible.

—Robert K. Corbin

Fire Over Texas

He made paperweights from inert hand grenade hulls and sold them at gun shows. It was a lucrative fund-raiser.[74]

If David Koresh was, in fact, a molester of children, this is not meant as a defense for his depravity, nor is it intended to endorse his interpretation of Christianity. It is only meant to show that he was marked for death by the United States Government as deliberately as John F. Kennedy was marked by his assassin.

Koresh (born Vernon Wayne Howell) bought and sold guns—or parts of guns—and other pyrotechnical paraphernalia as a means of raising money to help support his Branch Davidian Compound near Waco, Texas. He built knick-knacks and mounted wall plaques from hand grenade hulls, and even sold surplus military MREs (meals-ready-to-eat). His displays were popular at gun shows. He also assembled guns from gun parts and sold them through a licensed dealer. And he collected semi-automatic weapons as an investment, believing more stringent gun control laws would make them more valuable (as was the

---

[74] *Washington Post*, May 19, 1993, p. A19.

case when President Bush's ban on imports of such models caused their value to increase in 1989).[75]

There was also the consideration of self-protection. Koresh—certainly not your typical evangelist—received more than his share of hate mail. More significantly, there was direct contention for leadership of the Compound by George Roden. Koresh and some of his followers had reportedly exchanged gunfire with Roden some six years earlier, and Roden had threatened to return, saying, "I'm not going to come back with BB guns."[76]

In 1992, a United Parcel Service (UPS) driver reported to McLennan County authorities that he had delivered firearms components and "explosives" to a storage garage called "the Mag Bag" in Waco. On some occasions he was instructed to forward the deliveries on to David Koresh at Mount Carmel Center (the Branch Davidian Compound) for collection of C.O.D. charges. The driver reported seeing hand grenade hulls and a quantity of black powder (both items legal and largely unregulated) inside some damaged cartons.[77]

The Bureau of Alcohol, Tobacco and Firearms began an investigation of Koresh and some of his followers for possible firearms violations in June of 1992. The investigation soon zeroed in on Henry McMahon, proprietor of Hewitt Handguns where Koresh conducted most of his business. BATF agents Skinner and Aguilera found that Koresh had made purchases of flare launchers, over 100 rifles, an M-76 grenade launcher, various kits,

---

[75] Recorded interviews with licensed gun dealers Henry S. McMahon, Jr., and Karen J. Kilpatrick, Waco, TX, May 25, 1993, pp. 26, 108-109.

[76] McMahon and Kilpatrick interviews, 1993, pp. 105-106.

[77] "Affidavit to Kill," Paul H. Blackman, Ph.D., presented at the annual meetings of the American Society of Criminology, Phoenix, AZ, October 27-30, 1993, p. 4.

cardboard tubes, black powder, practice grenades, and more.[78] None of the items had been purchased illegally, however, and none established probable cause that Koresh had violated any federal law or that he even *intended* to.

The BATF and the media will not tell you Skinner and Aguilera were invited by David Koresh to visit his residence and inspect his weapons, or that the agents refused the offer. Nor was the incident included in the affidavit for search and arrest warrants. It happened as the agents poured over McMahon's records of firearms transactions. McMahon called Koresh on the phone and said, "... there (are) ATF agents at my house asking a lot of questions about (you)." Koresh said, "If there's a problem, tell them to come out here. If they want to see my guns, they're more than welcome." McMahon relayed the invitation, and Aguilera quickly refused the offer.[79]

The arrest and search warrant for Koresh, his residence, and others, was issued almost entirely on lies, misinformation, distortion of actual evidence and the ignorance of BATF agent Davy Aguilera.

The arrest warrant alleged that Koresh had violated §5845(f) of Title 26 of the U.S. Code, however, that provision only defines a "destructive device." It does not establish anything as a crime against the United States. It does not say it's unlawful to manufacture, possess, collect, use, admire or fondle destructive devices; it only *defines* them.[80]

---

[78] Application and Affidavit for Search and Arrest Warrants for Vernon Wayne Howell and the Residence of Vernon Wayne Howell, and others, Davy Aguilera, Waco, TX, February 25, 1993.

[79] *Soldier of Fortune*, "Waco: Behind the Cover-up," James L. Pate, November 1993, p. 37.

[80] U.S. Code, Title 26, Section §5845(f).

Aguilera listed as items to be searched for "machine-gun conversion parts, which, when assembled, would be classified as destructive devices," and items "which, when assembled, would be classified as destructive devices."[81] The affidavit *did not* list any actual machine guns or destructive devices among the items to be searched for. So, without probable cause to suggest a crime had been committed, BATF agents wanted to look for items that *when assembled* would become something illegal. (Perhaps federal agents should arrest everyone who owns a shotgun and a hacksaw.)

Aguilera said Koresh had ordered M16 "EZ kits," but never said *E2* kits were equally usable in semi-automatic Colt AR-15 Sporters, and with the legal purchase of regulated receivers, would allow the completion of an E2-model AR-15. The agent again misled Magistrate Dennis Green by referring to a "conversion kit" that is really a parts kit, and is not regulated by federal law. Aguilera claimed, in other cases, AR-15s had been easily converted into machine guns, using milling machines and lathes, thereby confusing the fabrication of a machine gun from a semi-automatic (requiring a great deal of expertise) with the installation of a conversion kit (requiring only assembly). The agent consistently misdescribed the conversion process, and (either from ignorance or a gross disregard for accuracy) failed to say that none of the "machine gun parts" allegedly delivered to Koresh were "conversion kits."[82]

Aguilera's statements before, during and after the deadly raid on the Branch Davidian Compound contained dozens of

---

[81] Application and Affidavit for Search and Arrest Warrants, Attachment D, Davy Aguilera, Waco, TX, February 25, 1993.

[82] "Affidavit to Kill," Paul H. Blackman, Ph.D., p. 12.

inaccuracies and untruths. Former associates of Koresh from within the Compound could not reliably testify as to whether the guns and pictures of guns they saw in Koresh's possession were legal semi-automatics or illegal machine guns. One so-called credible witness supported Aguilera's affidavit with testimony as flimsy as "... it was a machine gun because it functioned with a very rapid fire and tore up the ground when Howell shot it," and another said her brother "has some knowledge of firearms." The only time the investigation *might* have shown that Koresh purchased parts capable of converting semi-automatic firearms into machine guns, there was no follow-up on the lead. Amazingly, Aguilera determined "the sensitivity of this investigation" precluded his making contact with the only vendors who might have been able to incriminate Koresh.

Paul H. Blackman, Ph.D., of the National Rifle Association's Institute for Legislative Action, sums up the pre-raid investigation, which ultimately resulted in the deaths of 85 people:

> Overall, most of the allegations made in the affidavit by BATF's Aguilera, especially regarding the initial investigation, focused on Koresh during June-July 1992, dealt with the possibility that Koresh might have enough items to make hand grenades or other destructive devices, and had an interest in owning machine guns, and had some—but apparently not all—of the parts needed for conversion. Most of the affidavit's discussion of the acquisition of guns and parts suggested there was something wrong with the ownership of a large number of firearms *per se*, a view contrary to judicial decision (*United States* v. *Anderson*, 885 F.2d 1248 [5th Cir. 1989]) and federal statute (Firearms Owners' Protection Act of 1986, §1). Some of the firearms parts identified in the affidavit could have been used in either semi-automatic or full-auto firearms; some were

clearly semi-automatic, and duly purchased from licensed dealers. The only identified hand grenades were inert, since they were only hulls. So far as the affidavit's identification, no item listed as having been purchased by Koresh or his associates was purchased unlawfully, nor was it necessarily to be used unlawfully.[87]

At this point in the chronology, no one had been able to show that Vernon Wayne Howell, alias David Koresh, had committed a single offense, even one as minuscule as that of Randy Weaver cutting off a shotgun muzzle one-fourth of an inch too short. Having been unable to previously establish any "probable cause," the BATF infiltrated Special Agent Robert Rodriguez into Mount Carmel during the month of February. Rodriguez reported back to Davy Aguilera that Koresh had played the guitar for him, read from the Bible, and invited him to join the Davidians. Koresh allegedly warned Rodriguez that by joining the group he "would be disliked because the Government did not consider the group religious and that he (Koresh) did not pay taxes or local taxes because he felt he did not have to."

Aguilera included in his 15-page affidavit his own interpretation of "probable cause." He said Koresh had told Special Agent Rodriguez he believed in the right to bear arms, but said the U.S. Government planned to take that right away. Koresh reportedly spoke of the contradiction between a drop-in Sear for an AR-15 being legal and an AR-15 with the Sear being illegal. Koresh then showed Rodriguez a video made by Gun Owners of America portraying the ATF as an agency that violates gun owners' rights.[88]

---

[87] "Affidavit to Kill," p. 18.

[88] Application and Affidavit for Search and Arrest Warrants, Davy Aguilera, pp. 14-15.

(It appears that Koresh's most damning offense might have been telling the truth.)

Demonstrating his conviction that BATF needed to "get" Vernon Wayne Howell for *something*, Aguilera appealed to Magistrate Green, "I believe that Vernon Howell, also known as David Koresh, and/or his followers ... are unlawfully manufacturing and possessing machine guns and explosive devices." (All this without a shred of physical evidence—even with Special Agent Rodriguez *inside the compound!*)

Magistrate Green (relatively new to the bench, but having worked most of his legal career as a prosecutor) apparently did little or no homework on the application, granting Aguilera's requests pretty much carte blanche.

The initial raid on the Mount Carmel Center occurred February 28, 1993. Armed with a license to kill, obtained from Magistrate Green, 76 BATF agents stormed the compound. In the minutes that followed, four federal agents were killed and 14 to 28 others wounded—some of them almost certainly shot by one another. Six Branch Davidians were also killed and several others injured, including Koresh.

A 51-day standoff followed. The FBI replaced BATF in the leadership role. During that time, negotiation attempts were exchanged between Koresh and the federal authorities. Some adults and children left the compound. Agents implemented nuisance tactics (loud music, abrasive noises, taunting bullhorn messages) which totally violated hostage-negotiation protocol.

BATF agents went back to Magistrate Green for additional authorization to violate the rights of those individuals choosing to remain inside the compound. No one was ever able to say that a particular agent was shot by a particular Davidian, so Green issued another warrant giving agents authorization to search for cartridges, bullets, bullet holes, blood, and even video or audio tapes that might contain criticism "of firearms law enforcement and particularly the Bureau of Alcohol, Tobacco and Firearms" that would supposedly establish motive for shooting ATF agents.[89]

Meanwhile, an intense publicity blitz was begun by agency bureaucrats and the left-leaning media. The self-defense response of compound residents to the onslaught by dozens of heavily armed federal agents was turned into an "ambush" by NBC News, the BATF,[90] the Department of Treasury,[91] and the Department of Justice.[92] (It might also be noted that Polish soldiers were accused of *ambushing* Hitler's troops upon their invasion of Poland, and Custer's cavalry was *ambushed* by Indians after his columns had chased Sioux women and children along the Little Bighorn River.) The media heyday featured dozens of stories about Koresh's alleged perversions with young children of the compound, how he took other men's wives as his own, and with each passing day the compound "arsenal" seemed to grow and become more ominous.

---

[89] Application and Affidavit for Search Warrant for the Residence of Vernon Wayne Howell, and others, Earl Dunagan, Waco, TX, March 9, 1993, p. 4.

[90] Criminal Complaint and Affidavit, *U.S.A. v. Rita Faye Riddle*, Earl Dunagan, Waco, TX, April 18, 1993, p. 12.

[91] Report on the Bureau of Alcohol, Tobacco and Firearms Investigation of Vernon Wayne Howell also known as David Koresh, U.S. Department of the Treasury, Washington, D.C., Government Printing Office, September 1993, p. 100.

[92] Report on the Events at Waco, Texas, February 28 to April 19, 1993, Redacted Version, U.S. Department of Justice, Washington, D.C., October 8, 1993, p. 209.

Sheila Martin was inside the Mount Carmel Center on the morning of the attack. She and her three youngest children left the compound before the final assault, but her husband Wayne and their four teenagers stayed behind. The woman says David Koresh used to hold and soothe her son crippled with cerebral palsy and blindness for hours at a time. Martin says there was no ambush or any planned conspiracy to kill federal agents. She remembers hiding under a bed and crawling along a floor to get to her disabled son as bullets riddled her bedroom. She's haunted by her decision to leave the compound, and lives with the belief that her family will be reunited. She asks why a handicapped child would be left to sleep before a glass window if a shootout was expected. Sheila Martin adds, "There is no way there would have been just four agents killed if we were waiting for them. Our men were saving us from being killed."[93]

Only those who left the compound were assured of not being killed, however. Attorney General Janet Reno ordered the final assault, knowing at least 25 children were still inside. On April 19, 1993, CEV tanks began pounding holes in the walls and structures at Mount Carmel Center, pumping in CS gas. While armored combat vehicles rammed and rocked entire buildings, spitting nauseating tear gas into rooms containing babies, FBI Agent Byron Sage shouted over loudspeakers, "This is not an assault! Do not shoot. We are not entering your compound." Ambulances and local hospitals had been put on alert, and agents continued to call out, "You are responsible for your own actions.

---

[93] *U.S. News & World Report*, "One True Believer's Trials and Tribulations," Dan McGraw, January 17, 1994.

Come out now and you will not be harmed."[94] Sheila Martin's husband Wayne called 911 and pleaded, "Call them off—there are women and children in here!"[95] When the Davidians began firing in self-defense at the building-crunching tanks, federal agents became indiscriminate in spewing clouds of tear gas anywhere they could, irrespective of where women and children might have gathered for safety. Many had gone to a second-story location from which there was no exit.[96]

The Compound exploded and all but nine inside perished.

Many unproven allegations have been put forth from both sides of the controversy. Each side says the other shot first on February 28. Charges have come from within and without the BATF that agents were shot by other agents. Koresh supporters (and lawyers) say federal agents torched the Compound on April 19, while agents say it was murder/suicide committed by someone inside. Koresh and some others died from bullet wounds, some say self-inflicted, others allege otherwise. Government agencies involved engineered voluminous tidal waves of propaganda to cover errors that resulted in a badly botched initial raid and a poorly planned and managed resolution. BATF Director Stephen Higgins resigned, and Attorney General Janet Reno was elevated to bureau goddess status for accepting responsibility for the tragic outcome, and, at the same time, justifying the exchange of Davidian children's lives for BATF agents' lives. Some analysts likened David Koresh to Jim Jones, who led more than 900 of his

---

[94] *Time* Magazine, Special report, Nancy Gibbs, May 3, 1993, pp. 29-30.

[95] *Time* Magazine, "Another Judgment Day," Richard Lacayo, March 7, 1994, p. 45.

[96] *Time* Magazine, Special Report, May 3, 1993, p. 30.

own cult followers to their suicidal ends in 1978 at the People's Temple in Guyana.[97]

Many questions will never be answered; the incident will forever be debated. Why did federal agents train for months to assault an unorthodox religious compound when its leader could have been arrested dozens of times while jogging or shopping outside his residence?[98] Why was there a need for an "element of surprise" when Koresh had cooperated with authorities several times before, even turning himself and other Davidians in for arrest and surrender of weapons following the 1987 shootout with George Roden?[99] Why did Agent Aguilera pursue obtaining search and arrest warrants so relentlessly when there never was a preponderance of evidence to justify the push?

Koresh, wounded and holed up after the initial raid, said to an FBI negotiator, "It would have been better if you just called me up or talked to me ... Then you could have come in and done your work."[100]

Gun collectors with peculiar religious or political ideals are not popular with federal bureaucracies. In testimony before the House Judiciary Committee, then-BATF Director Higgins indicated that, although no evidence was available that Koresh had indeed converted semi-automatic rifles to machine guns or

---

[97] *Newsweek*, "Was It Friendly Fire?", April 5, 1993, p. 50; *Time* Magazine, Special report, May 3, 1993, pp. 32-33, 35; *Time* Magazine, "Amongst the Ashes," May 10, 1993, p. 22; *Newsweek*, "Sifting through the Ashes," May 10, 1993, p. 44: *Newsweek*, "The Book of Koresh," October 11, 1993, p. 27.

[98] *The New American*, "Truth and Cover-up: Sorting out the Waco Tragedy," Robert W. Lee, June 14, 1993, pp. 23-30.

[99] *The New American*, June 14, 1993, p. 23.

[100] *Washington Times*, May 26, 1993, p. A3.

made grenade hulls into live ones, the cult leader's views on religion and gun rights, his open criticism of federal gun laws and of the BATF, remained key elements in obtaining search and arrest warrants against him.[101] Higgins was scheduled to testify at congressional appropriations hearings during the second week of March, 1993. A successful raid on a radical cult compound, netting hundreds of semi-automatic ("assault") weapons, carried out only days before, certainly could not hurt a request for funding. An invitation to the national media might be helpful, too. Or was a diversion needed to draw attention away from allegations of sexual harassment within the BATF?[102]

A vigorous public relations campaign with national media cooperation turned the tide of public sentiment within weeks of the Waco holocaust. The BATF's mother Treasury Department conducted a self-cleansing investigation into the event, using its own agents from "other agencies." A resulting 500-page report—called the "Blue Book"—identified a circus of errors which led to the disaster and tragic loss of life on both sides. The report confirmed that agents had acted on sketchy information, had prepared poorly and, most damagingly, had allowed the initial raid to proceed even after learning they had lost the element of surprise.

No accountability for the blunders was ever laid on Stephen Higgins or Davy Aguilera or Magistrate Green. However, 11 Branch Davidians were subsequently charged with conspiracy to commit murder, voluntary manslaughter and weapon violations. Four of the defendants were completely exonerated. Two others were convicted on firearms charges. The five remaining

---

[101] "Affidavit to Kill," p. 27.
[102] *American Spectator,* "Gunning for Koresh, " Daniel Wattenberg, August 1993, p. 39.

men were found guilty of voluntary manslaughter and were sentenced to 40 years each in prison.[103]

Congressional hearings on the Waco incident, conducted during the summer of 1995, produced little more than another opportunity for the mainstream national media to compete for ratings. News cameras captured every moment of prepared testimony from a teenage girl who said she had been molested by David Koresh, then virtually ignored the statements of other surviving Davidians who clouded the claim. Involvement in the tragedy (plus Ruby Ridge) led to the FBI's Larry Potts being demoted from the second highest position in that agency. But no BATF personnel incurred disciplinary consequences. In fact, two raid leaders, who tried to blame their blunders on a younger undercover agent, were reinstated with full back pay.

Now, after six years of lies and cover-ups, the FBI still maintains they did not start the fire that killed 80 men, women and children at Waco. The pyrotechnic devices used by the FBI notwithstanding, the FBI knew that the only source of light and heat used by the Davidians was kerosene lamps. What did the FBI think would happen when they knocked over the walls of the Branch Davidian complex with a tank? After they did so, they blamed David Koresh for the fire.

The FBI also claims that the Davidians died as a result of a suicide pact promulgated by Koresh. Yet, all survivors of the Davidian inferno deny this claim. Even the Davidians who lost family members do not blame Koresh whatsoever. The Feds for six years have played the deny-and-blame game. They have learned well from the master how to dance the sidestep. Slick Willie should be so proud!

---

[103] *Newsweek*, March 7, 1994, p. 32; Associated Press, June 17, 1994.

From My Cold Dead Fingers

There is certainly a tendency for nations with restrictive gun laws to authorize additional powers to the police to violate the ordinary rights of privacy ... .

—Paul H. Blackman

History of a Natural Right

When James Madison drafted the Second Amendment, it was not based on some idea he created from thin air. British history—with which all the colonists were familiar—affirmed the right *and the duty* of every individual to own firearms. Sir William Blackstone, perhaps Britain's greatest common law interpreter, said the right to bear arms would allow citizens to vindicate all other rights.[104] The British right to bear arms was meant expressly to thwart unjust rulers, invading foreign governments and local crime. Not a word was written—nor thought given—about sporting purposes.

The original Colonies established a similar right and duty to bear arms. In 1658, the Virginia House of Burgesses *required* every householder to have a functioning firearm. That requirement was not so that all the colonists could get together on Sunday afternoons and target practice at the municipal range, nor was it so the male colonists could go camping for a week in autumn to drink beer, swap lies and chase trophy-antlered white-tails. It *was* for the purposes of assembling a militia of the citizenry to fight Indian wars (national security), to stand

---

[104] *Commentaries on the Laws of England*, I, William Blackstone, University of Chicago Press, Chicago, IL, 1979 (reprint), p. 139.

night-watch along the perimeters of some boroughs ("neighborhood watch"), to respond to the commands of sheriffs gathering posses to pursue outlaws (crime control), and to defend their homes, families and neighbors against thieves and marauders (self-defense).

The firearms used for these purposes by the colonists were "weapons of war." They were not guns designed for sporting events, although the same muskets and long-rifles were used by friendly shooters at marksmanship contests.

Without a cumulative "arsenal" of firearms among the colonists, the break with England would never have been conceived as a possibility—not to mention attained as a reality. As British soldiers increased their presence in the Colonies (and in the colonists' homes), the colonists turned to their firearms in order to defend their precious liberties. The *New York Journal Supplement* proclaimed in 1769, "It is a natural right which the people have reserved for themselves ... to keep arms for their own defense."[105]

British troops converged on Concord to seize an armory containing colonists' munitions, and the American Revolution began.[106] The experience of war with Britain reinforced the colonists' convictions that every freeman in America should keep and bear arms. American forces were ragged and scattered. They were farmers and hunters, merchants and builders. They assembled as militia and fought for their freedom wherever the British deployed. It became a classic (though unintentional) theater of guerilla warfare. American troops materialized from the boroughs and towns and remote countrysides, then melted away to

---

[105] "The 'Assault Weapon' Panic," Morgan and Kopel, p. 46.
[106] *Essex Gazette*, April 25, 1775, p. 3.

their shops and fields when a skirmish was over, making it virtually impossible for the more regimented British army to gain significant ground. Historian Daniel Boorstin said, "The American center was everywhere and nowhere—in each man himself."[107] After seven years of winning most of the battles and being no closer to victory, Britain gave up.

The American Revolution was won by a militia of citizens who had reserved for themselves the right to keep and bear arms. Retaining the capability to resist future federal oppression became a priority with the statesmen who framed the Constitution. Richard Henry Lee wrote "... the whole body of the people (should) always possess arms and be taught alike, especially when young, how to use them."[108] To allay fears sparked by Article I, Section 8, of the Constitution, granting Congress the power to "raise armies," Noah Webster wrote, "Before a standing army can rule, the people must be disarmed; as they are in almost every kingdom in Europe. The supreme power in America cannot enforce unjust laws by the sword; because the whole body of the people are armed ..."[109]

James Madison (who actually wrote the Second Amendment) saw the American government as unique in that "the ultimate authority ... resides in the people alone," as compared to European dictatorships "... afraid to trust the people with arms."[110]

---

[107] *The Americans: The Colonial Experience*, Daniel Boorstin, 1965.

[108] *Letters from the Federal Farmer to the Republican*, Richard Henry Lee.

[109] *Pamphlets on the Construction of the United States*, Noah Webster, 1888.

[110] *The Federalist*, James Madison, Number 46.

Alexander Hamilton declared, "If the representatives of the people betray their constituents, there is then no recourse left but in the exertion of that original right of self-defense which is paramount to all positive forms of government ..."[111]

Tench Coxe, a close friend of Madison, proclaimed, "The powers of the sword are in the hands of the yeomanry of America from sixteen to sixty. The militia of these free commonwealths, entitled and accustomed to their arms, when compared with any possible army, must be tremendous and irresistible. Who are the militia? Are they not ourselves...? Congress have no power to disarm the militia."[112]

Patrick Henry stated without equivocation: "Guard with jealous attention the public liberty. Suspect everyone who approaches that jewel. Unfortunately, nothing will preserve it but downright force. Whenever you give up that force, you are ruined ... The great object is that every man be armed ... Everyone who is able may have a gun."[113]

This might be a good time to ask a few important questions. Does it not seem today that our American Government is "... afraid to trust the people with arms?" And if so, why? Could it be "the representatives of the people" *know* they have "betray[ed] their constituents," and intend to further do so? Is there any debate left over *who* the "militia of these free commonwealths" (states) really are? The founders of our young nation did not write their prophetic manifestoes in reference to duck-hunting or trapshooting firearms; they were referring directly to

---

[111] *The Federalist*, Alexander Hamilton, Number 28.

[112] *Pennsylvania Gazette*, Tench Coxe, February 20, 1788.

[113] *The Antifederalist Papers*, Morton Borden, Michigan State University Press, East Lansing, MI, vol. 3, p. 386.

"weapons of war." Keeping Americans armed with weapons sufficient to discourage government tyranny was a condition the first statesmen intended to remain intact. They provided no authority to a federal congress to ever tamper with it. How many "yeomanry of America from sixteen to sixty" today are willing and prepared to "preserve it (with) downright force?"

Perhaps another question should be addressed to our nation's education system in general. Why is it that the views of the Founding Fathers regarding gun control and the Second Amendment are nowhere to be found in our schools' history books? Are we afraid to teach our children the truth? Or would these truths have a destructive effect on the plan to move our future citizens away from American idealism?

Washington powercrats today take much comfort in the complacency of American citizens. The misconception that the Federal Government is *THE* superior omnipotent "being" serves as a big security cushion around those who believe they can lead this nation into a New World Order under command of the United Nations without resistance from the people. (They just might do it, too!) They believe an American public conditioned to perceive the Federal Government as too powerful to resist will tolerate any conditions they might decide to impose.

(Are they right?)

A part of the plan is to make property rights meaningless through environmental controls. Then comes a weakening of the free enterprise system by allowing government to control the water and minerals, forests and oil reserves. The plan is simplified when *everybody* arrives on a level playing field known as "socialized medicine," with no distinctions between the rich and poor, young and old, the weak and powerful.

These things are all being done, very effectively, by Washington and world strategists—with *little concerted resistance from the people!* There are other glaring signs: a crime bill that authorizes the hiring of Hong Kong Royalty Police in America;[114] a New Age president offering condolences in the death of North Korean despot Kim Il Sung "on behalf of the American people;"[115] an FBI office in Moscow, Russia, working on *Russian* organized crime;[116] American troops under U.N. command in "peace-keeping" efforts all over the globe; a United Nations Covenant granting control of civil and political rights to *".. procedures ... established by the [international] law".*[117]

An armed America still believing in the U.S. Constitution and the Bill of Rights is not conducive to totalitarian leadership. Socialistic politicians believe *they* can "take care of" the American people better than the American people can. To accomplish this, however, the people must be totally dependent upon the government—for employment, enterprise, health care, welfare and other entitlements. An umbrella of control opens, then, over the lives of individual citizens. The single circumstance needed to facilitate complete government dominance is the removal of guns from the hands and homes of all Americans. The same logic led to broad confiscation of guns by an array of disparate dictators from around the world—Ferdinand Marcos, Fidel Castro, Idi Amin, and the Bulgarian Communists.[118]

---

[114] S.17091, Section §5108.

[115] Associated Press, July 11, 1994.

[116] FBI Report, as heard on Rush Limbaugh radio show, EIB Network, July 12, 1994.

[117] United Nations Covenant on Civil and Political Rights, United States Senate, ratified August 1991, passed with unrecorded vote April 2, 1992.

[118] "The 'Assault Weapon' Panic," Morgan and Kopel, p. 63.

In conclusion, gun control is a single link in a long chain of political and social agendas all connected to pull the American public into democratic socialism. *Public* political rationale on the issue is hollow and dishonest. Emotional (political and public) responses to societal trends or traumatic events are superficial and dangerous. Private anti-gun crusades led by clever spinmasters (Bill Peters of KABC) and misinformed mouthpieces (Sarah Brady of HCI) are an undertow sucking at basic civil rights. On a mission to sanctify every objective of the liberal leadership in Washington, the national mainstream media undermines Americanism. To tamper with the tenets of the U.S. Constitution and Bill of Rights is to risk the very essence of freedom.

Gun control legislation is unconstitutional; it was never intended as an option. A federal government becoming more and more powerful by self-authorization, however, has good reason to be nervous about freemen of the several states armed to the teeth and ready to take it on. What better reason (in the mind of government, anyway) to alter the basis for that ever-present threat of civil rebellion?

Preservation of freedom in the United States of America has fallen on the shoulders of armed citizens for more than 220 years.

It still does.

The powers not delegated to the United States by the Constitution, nor prohibited by it to the States, are reserved to the States respectively, or to the people.

—U.S. Constitution, Tenth Amendment

II

Fallacies and Facts

We are freeing men from the responsibilities of freedom, which only a few men can bear.

—Adolph Hitler

Citizens and Guns

Cliff Milton knew he and his wife Dottie would be killed that night. The elderly couple were enjoying a quiet evening in their family room when Marcus Esparza burst in. Big and unshaven, the man's appearance was intimidating—even without the pistol he trained at Cliff Milton's heart.

"I want your money and your jewelry," Esparza said.

Cliff was afraid, but mostly for Dottie, his wife and companion of 50 years. The man in his house had come with a handgun and a plan to rob two apparently helpless residents of a peaceful north Dallas neighborhood. Cliff considered jumping the man and giving Dottie a chance to escape, but he knew she wouldn't run. And Cliff had had prostate surgery only five days earlier. He knew he and Dottie would die at the hands of a criminal covering his tracks.

He cooperated and gave the man his money. Dottie handed over a gold necklace. Cliff tried to reason with the man, that he would try to help him if he would put down the gun. The man scoffed.

Esparza ordered the Miltons upstairs. Cliff saw the muzzle of the pistol pressed against Dottie's spine. In an upstairs bedroom, Cliff sat down on a bed and explained he was suffering with cancer.

The thief muttered, "... it won't be so bad if I kill you; you're gonna die anyhow." He then demanded Cliff's guns.

Cliff surrendered a .357 Magnum revolver and a .22 pistol, looking for any opportunity to trick the gunman. It never came. Cliff and Dottie were herded back to the family room and forced to sit on a couch.

The gunman said, "I'm going to kill your wife first." He cocked and pointed Cliff's .22.

Cliff Milton lunged from the couch, jamming the heel of his left hand into the space between the gun's hammer and firing pin. He struggled with more strength than he knew he possessed, throwing the intruder off balance. He felt the hammer of the pistol chewing at his hand as the gunman repeatedly tried to fire. Dottie dashed for the phone. Esparza lost his grip on the .22, and Cliff turned the gun on him.

"Shoot me!" the man sneered. "I'm not going back to prison!" And he took a threatening step forward.

Dottie suddenly appeared holding the .357 Magnum at arm's length, cocked and steady. Esparza abandoned his bluff. The 70-year-olds—*armed with their own pistols*—held their would-be killer at bay until police arrived.

(Marcus Anthony Esparza was fined $30,000 and sentenced to life in prison as a paroled felon convicted of two counts of first-degree aggravated robbery with a deadly weapon and another burglary charge. Cliff Milton was awarded the prestigious Citizens Certificate of Merit by Dallas police.)[1]

The story of Cliff and Dottie Milton is not unique in very many ways—perhaps only in that Cliff Milton was recovering from surgery and still overpowered Esparza, or that a 70-year-

---

[1] *Reader's Digest*, "He's Going to Kill Us!", Mary Murray, June 1994, pp. 41-46.

old unarmed man was able to wrestle a weapon from the grasp of a strapping young intruder. But private citizens in America do, indeed, defend themselves against criminal attack hundreds of thousands of times every year. A Florida State University criminologist says, "... gun ownership must surely be considered a very routine aspect of American life and of obvious relevance to the activities of criminals."

Dr. Gary Kleck—who became an advocate of gun ownership only after conducting extensive studies on the topic— estimates there were about 645,000 defensive uses of handguns against potentially dangerous aggressors in 1988, excluding incidents involving police and military personnel. That does not include the same kinds of incidents with private citizens using rifles. Kleck said then, "... guns of all types are used for defensive purposes about one million times a year." He added, "Guns of all types are used substantially more often defensively than criminally."[2]

(That deserves repeating!)

Guns of all types are used substantially more often defensively than criminally.

Five years later—in his National Self-Defense Survey— Kleck upped the estimate to as many as 2,500,000 crimes thwarted each year in America by private citizens using firearms. This was not written by some militant extremist crackpot; Professor Gary Kleck is a most-respected researcher, criminologist and author. He is the ultimate skeptic and will leave no stone unturned in collecting and verifying data. His book *Point Blank: Guns and Violence in America* is an undisputed resource on crime, violence and firearm statistics, and retails for more than $150.

---

[2] *Social Problems*, "Crime Control Through the Private Use of Armed Force," Gary Kleck, February 1988.

Kleck belongs to the American Civil Liberties Union, Amnesty International USA, Common Cause, and other politically liberal groups. He has never belonged or contributed to the NRA, HCI, or any other group on either side of the gun-control issue. Neither has he accepted research funding from any gun (or gun-control) advocacy group. When Gary Kleck reports that "... guns of all types are used substantially more often defensively than criminally," it is not a statement of conjecture. Why, then, are these incidents not reported on the evening news? Because private citizens throttling criminal activity *before* it happens in their homes and neighborhoods does not make headlines as colorful as gang murders and school yard shootings. Bill Peters at KABC-TV and *Time* magazine don't care about statistics that challenge their agendas.

The 1988 Kleck study found that although shootings of criminals by citizens represent only a fraction of overall defensive uses of guns, private Americans shoot criminals dead as many as seven times more frequently than police do. (That's called a "deterrent!") Kleck goes on, "... there were about 8,700-16,000 non-fatal, legally permissible woundings of criminals by gun-armed civilians."[3]

A Justice Department survey found that from a total 32,000 attempted rapes, 32 percent were actually committed. However, when a potential rape victim "was armed with a gun or knife, only 3 percent of the attempted rapes were successful."[4]

While liberal anti-gunners claim firearms owned for protection are not only "useless," but "dangerous to the victim," Dr.

---

[3] *Social Problems*, "Crime Control Through the Private Use of Armed Force," Gary Kleck, February 1988.

[4] *Journal of the Medical Association of Georgia*, Edgar A Suter, M.D., March 1994, p. 149.

Kleck uproots that fallacy, using victimization surveys commissioned by the U.S. Department of Justice. Government-funded reports verify "for both robbery and assault, victims who used guns for protection were less likely either to be attacked or injured than victims who responded in *any other way* (emphasis added), including those who did not resist at all." Only 12 percent of victims resisting assault by using a gun, and 17 percent resisting robbery, suffered any kind of injury. The next safest recourse was passivity (doing nothing to resist). Twenty-five to 27 percent of assault and robbery victims choosing this method of defense were injured anyway. (Refer to graph on p. 89.)

A most effective crime deterrent is the criminals' perception of armed victims. University of Massachusetts sociological researchers James Wright and Peter Rossi interviewed nearly 2,000 imprisoned felons in ten different states, and determined two things very quickly. First, gun control laws had virtually no effect on the availability of guns to criminals, but, most interestingly, the study confirmed that 56 percent of the criminals would not attack a potential victim known to be armed. Further, 74 percent said burglars avoid houses where people are at home because they "fear being shot during the crime." Thirty-nine percent of the interviewed felons had personally decided *not* to commit at least one crime because they had reason to believe their intended victim might have a gun, and eight percent said the experience had happened "many times." Thirty-four percent of them said they had actually been scared off, shot at, wounded or captured by an armed citizen.[5]

---

[5] *The Armed Criminal in America*, James W. Wright and Peter H. Rossi, National Institute of Justice of the U.S. Justice Department, 1985.

Gary Kleck feels the Wright-Rossi study is inherently flawed by a reluctance on the part of hardened criminals to admit to being "scared off" by victims. Kleck concurs, however, that "these quasi-experiments ... do support the argument that routine gun ownership and defensive use by civilians has an ongoing impact on crime ..."[6]

(What was that! ... *gun ownership and defensive use by civilians has an ongoing impact on crime...*? How can that be when firearms owned for self-protection are not only "useless," but "dangerous to the [owner] victim?")

Catherine Latta of Charlotte, North Carolina, would argue the point. In September of 1990, Charlotte tried to get permission from local police to buy a handgun for protection from an ex-boyfriend who had previously beaten, robbed and raped her. A sheriff's clerk explained she would have to wait from two to four weeks for a permit.

She said, "I'll be dead by then."

Later that day she bought a gun illegally—a semi-automatic pistol for $20 from a "vendor" on the street. A few hours later, the man she feared most attacked her where she lived, and she shot him dead. A sensible county prosecutor refused to bring charges against her for either shooting her attacker or possession of an illegal gun.

Bonnie Elmasri *cannot* argue the point. The Wisconsin woman called a firearms instructor for advice on obtaining a handgun in March of 1991. She said her husband (already under court order to stay away) was threatening her and her two children. The instructor explained Wisconsin had a 48-hour waiting

---

[6] *America Rifleman*, "Armed Citizens & Crime Control," Paul H. Blackman, Ph.D., July 1988.

period. Twenty-four hours later, Bonnie Elmasri and her children were murdered by the man she feared most.[7]

Incidents of citizens protecting themselves when the police were not there are many. A group of Cambodians at a housing project in Los Angeles used M-1s and Kalashnikovs to put down an attack by the Bloods in May of 1988.[8] Drug dealers terrorized Piru Street in Los Angeles until two gang members were shot and wounded by a "block watch" leader, attracting the attention of police.[9] Korean merchants protected their property during the 1992 Los Angeles riots with "assault weapons."[10] Off-duty Army Rangers launched a "free-fire" offensive against crack-cocaine dealers in Tacoma, Washington, using handguns, shotguns and semi-automatic rifles, and driving the drug dealers from their streets.[11] Property owners have taken up arms to protect their property following most natural disasters, including Florida hurricanes, Midwest flooding and California earthquakes. Gary Kleck insists Americans use handguns (not rifles or other models) for defense against crime and aggression at least every 48 seconds.[12]

In the face of overwhelming evidence proving the inefficacy of gun control laws, anti-gun organizations and politicians continue to work toward broader bans, increased regulation, tighter control. "Control" is the key word here—control of the private lives of American citizens. Twenty thousand gun control

---

[7] *Policy Review,* "The Violence of Gun Control," David B. Kopel, Winter 1993, pp. 5-6.

[8] *Los Angeles Times,* May 13, 1988.

[9] *Washington Times,* November 25, 1988, p. C6.

[10] "The 'Assault Weapon' Panic," Morgan and Kopel, p. 60.

[11] *Rocky Mountain News,* September 29, 1989, p. 4.

[12] *Policy Review,* "The Violence of Gun Control," Kopel, Winter 1993, p. 3.

laws have not worked. Not a single piece of evidence can be shown that even *one* of those laws prevented a single crime or act of violence. Making possession of firearms illegal does not work, nor do random "stop-and-frisk" searches as done in the streets, shops and restaurants of Belfast, Ireland. People there still possess, carry and use guns.[13]

The United States of America was born with a gun in her hand. The blood in her veins flows with the resilient spirit of freedom-loving countrymen (and women) in her cities, mountains and fruited plains. For more than two centuries her sons and daughters have defended themselves, their loved ones, their properties and the borders of their motherland with guns. Only a government out of control with self-authorization of power could view the principles of freedom with such disdain as to want to eliminate them. Only a government bent on totalitarian control would strive to turn the people of a nation into defenseless "subjects."

Only a nation of armed citizens—the ones who protect themselves from criminal attack every 48—seconds is equipped of mind, spirit and arsenal sufficient to protect the intent of the Founding Fathers and the tenets of the U.S. Constitution and Bill of Rights. As a united people, we must not allow the enemy to take away our last argument for freedom.

---

[13] National Public Radio, "All Things Considered," March 8, 1979.

Those who would sacrifice liberty for safety will have neither liberty nor safety.

—Benjamin Franklin

From My Cold Dead Fingers

We can't be so fixated on our desire to preserve the rights of ordinary Americans to legitimately own handguns and rifles ... that we are unable to think about reality.

—Bill Clinton

Lawmakers' Ruse

As mentioned earlier in this book, when legislators in Washington introduce cumbersome volumes of (unconstitutional) legislation disguised as a prescription for some epidemic social malady, they will attempt to justify their "benevolence" with a frightening preamble. The information presented is often distorted with "facts" clearly designed to enhance passage of the bill.

A good way to illustrate this might be to look at a piece of legislation as actually presented by lawmakers. In May of 1993, a bill was introduced before the U.S. Senate to prohibit the manufacture, importation, exportation, sale, purchase, transfer, receipt, possession, or transport of handguns and handgun ammunition, with certain exceptions. In justifying yet another swipe at constitutional liberty, the preamble to S.892 stated:

"... the number of privately held handguns has more than doubled—from 33,000,000 in 1973 to more than 70,000,000 today—in the past two decades alone, and the number of handguns in circulation continues to increase by 2,000,000 handguns each year ...;" [14]

---

[14] S.892, In the Senate of the United States, May 5 (legislative day April 19), 1993, preamble paragraph 1.

(So what! Americans have a right to keep and bear arms. Only a small fraction of these handguns are in the possession of criminals. Most are owned and kept by the law-abiding private sector as a major deterrent to crime, and as the absolute guarantee against government tyranny.)

Sponsoring lawmakers also declared: "... *the number of handgun homicides has set new records every year since 1987, matching pace with the skyrocketing national homicide rate ...;*"[15]

(An absurd statement. Why should it be any other way? And if this is justification for banning handguns, then why are we not seeing legislation proposing bans on all other types of weapons that contribute to the "national homicide rate?" Doesn't simple logic suggest that if handgun homicides and the national homicide rate are only "matching pace," then knife homicides or tire iron homicides or necktie homicides must also be setting "new records" to round out the spectrum?)

Contrary to voluminous statistics, independent studies and *government-funded* surveys showing the consistent frequency and value of private citizens protecting themselves with their own guns, the authors of S.892 pressed stubbornly onward: "... *handguns kept in the home are of less value than is commonly thought in defending against intruders, and they are far more likely to increase significantly the danger of a handgun fatality or injury to the inhabitants (including children) than to enhance their personal safety ...;*"[16]

(Cliff Milton and hundreds of thousands more know better. And while gun control advocates say 1,000 kids are accidentally shot to death in their homes each year, they cannot pro-

---

[15] S.892, preamble paragraph 3.
[16] S.892, preamble paragraph 6.

duce the data to prove it. Meanwhile, the National Safety Council says 277 children under age 15 were accidentally killed by guns in 1988, and the National Center for Health Statistics says that number decreased to 236 in 1990.[17] The number of kids killed in automobile and motorcycle accidents exceeds the number killed in gun-related accidents dozens-fold. In rural areas where kids are raised with a knowledge of guns from an early age, firearms rate lower than farm animals and machinery in occurrences of fatal accidents.)

"... violent crime and injury committed with handguns constitute a burden upon and interfere with interstate and foreign commerce, and threaten the domestic tranquility of the Nation;"[18]

(So does "violent crime and injury" committed with *anything!*)

"... current Federal firearms policy is wholly inadequate to counteract the social, economic, and financial costs exacted by handguns to our society."[19]

(Current "Federal firearms policy" is wholly *unconstitutional*, and will never be an effective treatment or cure for "social, economic, and financial" turbulence *of any kind!*)

Lawmakers try to condition (brainwash) an uninformed and gullible American public by toying with their emotions. One way to do that is to present staggering statistics that will ultimately affect them financially. S.892 claimed: *"... handgun vio-*

---

[17] "Children and Guns: Sensible Solutions," David B. Kopel, Independence Institute, Golden, CO, April 25, 1993, p. 5.

[18] S.892, preamble paragraph 7.

[19] S.892, preamble paragraph 8.

lence places considerable strain on the national health care system and is a major contributor to its escalating costs, with at least $4,000,000,000 being spent annually on emergency care, hospitalization, follow-up care, rehabilitation, and medication;"[20]

(Don't forget the enormous scope of this legislation—to totally ban handguns and handgun ammunition. Therefore, they must present a scenario of justification equally as encompassing. Health care costs are important to everyone. So let's scare hell out of the American public with erroneous claims and statistics. Perhaps the public will then be less frightened by the prospect of being disarmed and won't bother to check the "facts." While the anti-gun legislators claim $4,000,000,000 are being spent annually to treat gunshot victims, the actual figure is more like $2,000,000,000—still a lot of money. However, it represents about one-fourth of one percent of America's $800,000,000,000 annual medical bill. Further, the legislators fail to say about $5,000,000,000—two and a half times the cost of gunshot treatment—are spent treating blood infections that occur *inside hospitals*, and that 30,000 deaths occur annually as the result of these "in-house" infections. That's only 7,000 fewer than all the gun-caused fatalities in the whole nation for the same period of time.[21] When will we see legislation proposing bans on blood syringes and IV needles?)

Of course, the most effective lever applied to human emotion always deals with kids. Rational, practical, intelligent adults are often willing to make irrational, impractical and completely

---

[20] S.892, preamble paragraph 5.

[21] Statistics from the *International Journal of Epidemiology*, and presented in a National Rifle Association Institute for Legislative Action Fact Sheet.

foolish sacrifices if they are convinced it'll be "good for the kids." Manipulative lawmakers turn this to their own advantage, using generalized rhetoric and innuendo as statements of fact: "... *the number of handgun-related incidents in elementary and secondary schools has increased sharply, with significant numbers of schoolchildren in rural and urban areas reporting easy access to and frequent carrying to school of handguns; and the presence of handguns in school not only provokes worry among parents and children but also causes much needed school funds to be diverted for purchase of security equipment ...;*"[22]

(So has the numbers of *students* in schools "increased sharply." How many are "significant numbers?" What "rural and urban areas?" The "presence" of alcohol and drugs and potential sex offenders also "provokes worry among parents and children," and "causes much needed school funds to be diverted for purchase of security equipment." No amount of federal gun regulation is going to keep guns out of schools. A very large portion of the firearms showing up at schools are obtained illegally—the same as contraband drugs and alcohol—and federal regulation will not change that. If anything, when every law-abiding American has been disarmed, the black-market availability of guns will become so rampant that many *more* students will acquire them for self-protection.)

It's all a ruse. The motivation behind Washington lawmakers' efforts to pass still more ineffective and illegal gun control laws is not to reduce the crime rate because they *know* it will not. Neither do they believe there will be a resultant impact on acts of violence or incidents of suicide because impassioned people employ whatever "tools" are available. Concern for kids

---

[22] S.892, preamble paragraph 4.

is a lie because the true bases for escalating social problems in schools are not being addressed.

Washington powercrats want to create an unarmed nation. It's all pretty simple. They are uneasy about a gun-toting constituency that believes in a constitutional right *and duty* to resist oppressive federal government. They continually assume additional power not granted them by the Constitution. Efforts to repeal the Second Amendment are underway. Having lost all regard for the convictions and deeds of founding colonists who gambled their lives on the creation of the most unique nation on earth, Washington socialists today are looking for a smooth and easy transition to a New World Order. United Nations troops are training to confiscate American guns. U.S. Navy Seals and Marine Corps troops are being asked to consider an oath of allegiance to the United Nations.[23]

Some early gun laws (i.e., banning machine guns in 1934 in response to organized crime activities of the Depression Era), may have been enacted with honorable intentions. Proposed antigun legislation today is so much broader, and contains powerful and dangerous implications. Health care costs and suicides and guns at schools are simply "surrogate" issues aimed at furthering subversive political agendas. And there continues an unending tide of them.

A day of reckoning is inevitable. Will guns be outlawed and taken away, leaving little vestige of constitutional freedom? Armed Americans (hopefully) will not submit willingly. On the other hand, a disarmed citizenry will have no choice but to behave like sheep. The pioneers of freedom who wrote the Declaration of Independence were considered traitors by a despotic

---

[23] *Napa Sentinel*, The Magazine & North American Investigative Journal, Harry Martin, July 1994.

British government, but they were not sheep. Neither did they intend their descendants to be.

Personal liberties and unalienable rights as guaranteed by the United States Constitution and Bill of Rights are in grave danger. Some are gone; others are eroding rapidly. Only a united resistance in the spirit of traditional patriotism will preserve those remaining and begin to restore those already lost.

Or have we become a nation of sheep?

Mack is thus forced to choose between violating his oath or violating the Act, subjecting himself to possible sanctions.

—Judge John Roll, ruling in *Mack* v. *U.S.*, 1994

Truth about Kids and Guns

Misinformation about kids and guns is profuse. It comes from the left-leaning media, from ambitious politicians, from innumerable agencies, organizations and public figures. They all are draped with a veil of credibility. Therefore, gross misstatements become accepted as facts. Some examples:

"One child under 14 is accidentally shot to death every day in the USA."
—Center to Prevent Handgun Violence

"Teen-agers in homes with guns are 75 times more likely to kill themselves than teenagers living in homes without guns."
—*Washington Post* columnist Richard Reeves

"In the past decade, more than 138,000 Americans were shot by children under the age of 6."
—*Hartford Courant*

"135,000 children carry guns to school each day."
—Senators Joseph Biden and John Chafee

"Firearms are responsible for the deaths of 45,000 infants, children and adolescents per year."
—American Academy of Pediatrics

"One million U.S. inhabitants die prematurely each year as the result of intentional homicide or suicide."
—former U.S. Surgeon General C. Everett Koop

"Guns are the leading cause of death among older teenagers—white and black—in America."
—*Newsweek*

These statistics are frightening and *false*—every one of them! Therefore, we are going to take a detailed look at the emotional and often distorted issue of kids and guns.

David B. Kopel, Director of the Second Amendment Project at the Independence Institute in Golden, Colorado, has done

---

[24] All examples compiled in "Children and Guns: Sensible Solutions," David B. Kopel, Independence Institute, Golden, CO, April 25, 1993, p. 4.

[25] David B. Kopel also serves as an associate policy analyst with the Cato Institute in Washington, DC. He is author of the book *The Samurai, the Mountie, and the Cowboy: Should America Adopt the Gun Controls of other Democracies?* (Prometheus Books, Buffalo, NY, 1992), and was awarded the Comparative Criminology Prize by the American Society of Criminology's Division of Comparative and International Criminology. Much of the chapter "Truth about Kids and Guns" is taken from a study (named in footnote 24) by Kopel. Some additional footnotes will indicate Kopel's sources.

[26] The Independence Institute is a nonprofit, nonpartisan Colorado think tank. It is governed by a statewide board of trustees and holds 501(c)(3) tax exemption from the IRS. The Institute focuses on social and political issues from human rights and economics to education reform, government, and the environment.

extensive research to try and reflect a more realistic light on the emotional issue of kids and guns. Kopel found, contrary to the propaganda of the prohibitionist group Center to Prevent Handgun Violence, in 1990, 34 children under age five died in gun accidents. Fifty-six children from ages five to nine were accidentally shot to death, and children ten to 14 suffered 146 fatal accidents. A dramatic decline in fatal gun accidents involving children (nearly 50 percent) occurred in the two decades since 1970, even as the number of firearms owned by Americans rose to 200,000,000 (a third of them handguns).

Further, the overall fatal gun accident rate for the American population has been declining more rapidly than rates for other types of accidental deaths. From 1968 to 1988, the fatal gun accident rate fell from 1.2 per 100,000 people in a year to 0.6—a decline of 50 percent. Job site fatalities declined by 47 percent, and motor vehicle fatalities decreased by only 27 percent.

It's only appropriate to point out the Occupational Safety and Health Administration is devoted to reducing work-related accidents. The U.S. Department of Transportation and numerous state agencies and other organizations work to make motorists safer. *There is no government agency dedicated to reducing firearms accidents.* The reduction in firearms accidents can only be attributed to the voluntary educational efforts sponsored and provided by groups like the National Rifle Association, the Boy Scouts, 4-H and others.

Graphs on the next page illustrate the significant declines in fatal gun accidents involving children 14 and under, and the American population overall.

---

[27] *Accident Facts: 1992 Edition*, National Safety Council, Itasca, IL, 1992, p. 22.

[28] *Accident Facts: 1992 Edition*, pp. 33, 37.

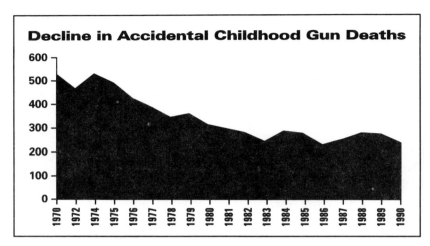

The number of fatal gun accidents involving children has fallen by over 50%, even as the number of guns and the number of children have increased.

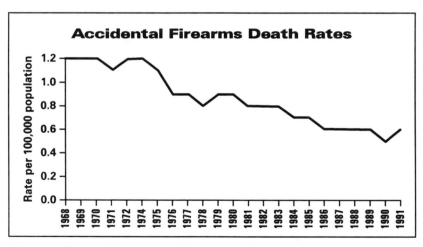

The overall rate of fatal gun accidents has fallen by 50%. About one person in 200,000 will die in a gun accident in an average year.

Probably no other cause of childhood death has fallen more sharply than death by accidental shooting, and the decline has occurred without the aid of any government program designed to reduce accidents. Many observers say this is a strong argument for more private safety programs and less government regulation, and certainly that no persuasive case exists for restrictive gun controls designed to fight gun accidents among children.

Some anti-gunners, however, continue to push for tighter gun controls, *claiming* to deal with the issue of accidents. Again, they're on the wrong road to nowhere because their successes will only shoot more holes (no pun intended) in the Second Amendment and do nothing to reduce accidental deaths. Gun control advocates do little to learn the true facts on most issues, or to help spread them, because the truth would serve only to undermine their mission. Actual numbers are readily available from *government* statistics. Still, gun control advocates talk about accidents and fatalities in ways that avoid mentioning verifiable numbers. Gun control organizations actually *oppose* safety education programs while supporting laws that will impair the rights of all gun owners.

The *Journal of the American Medical Association* states simply that a "firearm in the home" is a risk factor for home firearm accidents. A true statement, of course, but only because the topic is firearms. The same thing could have been written about swimming pools, trampolines, skateboards, or Doberman pinschers. The very low rate of child deaths attributed to gun accidents certainly clouds the *Journal*'s assertion.

David Kopel says if guns should be outlawed because they contribute to 236 accidental childhood deaths a year, then so should bicycles (the cause of over 400 child deaths a year) or automobiles (which kill more than 3,260 kids annually).[29] Additionally, 432 children die each year in accidental fires caused by adults falling asleep while smoking; 350 kids under five drown in bathtubs and swimming pools; and 90 more in the same age group are killed with cigarette lighters (only 34 in the under-five group are killed with guns). Kopel points out that owners of swimming pools, bathtubs, automobiles, bicycles, tobacco and cigarette lighters have no constitutional right to possess those items, none of which do a thing to save lives or prevent assault and injury.

Some gun owners lock their firearms away, with corresponding ammunitions kept under separate lock at some other location, and the keys hidden independently of one another. Of course, under these conditions, protecting oneself from an unwanted intruder is reduced to the equivalent of having no gun at all. "Trigger locks" are available. These are simple devices that prevent a gun from firing until the lock is removed with a key. However, being forced by government mandate to use such devices impairs the constitutional guarantee that firearms may be kept for self-protection because a gun with a "trigger lock" is not readily usable in the event of emergency.

Awareness and safety education are still the best weapons against accidental gun-related deaths of children. After a Colorado teenager accidentally shot her brother to death at a party, one parent lamented, "We talked to our kids about AIDS, about school, about drugs—but not guns."[30] Parents have a responsibility to talk with their children about all the potential dangers in their lives—alcohol and AIDS, swimming pools (even when they don't own one), automobiles, "friendly" strangers, *and guns!*

---

[29] *Accident Facts: 1992 Edition*, pp. 22, 65.

[30] *Denver Post*, September 26, 1991, p. B1.

It goes much further than "child-proofing" firearms; it means "accident-proofing" children.

On the subject of suicide, columnist Richard Reeves of the *Washington Post* wrote that kids living in homes with guns are 75 times more likely to kill themselves. His statement was based on grossly flawed information that was later repudiated by its creator.[31] The study was conducted only on homes in western Pennsylvania occupied by teenagers with known psychiatric/ suicide problems. There was no examination of data collected from homes with apparently normal teenagers not suffering from psychiatric conditions. Still, the erroneous report printed in the *Journal of the American Medical Association* has remained the basis for inaccurate journalism and proposed legislation to further ban guns. Even Senator John Chafee of Rhode Island repeated the "75-fold" figure to a congressional committee in 1992, giving no notice to the *Journal*'s retraction.

Chafee and Reeves are not the only ones spreading misinformation about teen suicide. The American Academy of Pediatrics told a congressional committee in 1989, "Every three hours, a teenager commits suicide with a handgun." The Education Fund to End Gun Violence, and Handgun Control, Inc. repeat the "every-three-hours" claim, applying it to "firearms" rather than just handguns.

Either way, the assertion is false. "Every three hours" becomes more accurate when applied to *all* suicides (no matter the method), or if statistics include every suicide up to *age 25*

---

[31] *Journal of the American Medical Association*, "The Presence and Accessibility of Firearms in the Homes of Adolescent Suicides: A Case-Controlled Study," David A. Brent, J.A. Perper, C.J. Allman, G.M. Moritz, M.E. Wartella, J.P. Zelenak, 1991, pp. 2989-2995.

(certainly not teenagers). The teenage suicide-by-gun rate is only *half* what the anti-gun groups claim.[32]

A graph on the next page shows a steady rise in teen suicide incidents from the mid sixties to the late seventies, and a fairly stable rate since. Many reasons that might account for the sixties/seventies climb are up for speculation—drugs, Vietnam, widespread social unrest, a breakdown of moral values. Some "experts" will attach the increase to a corresponding increase in firearms, but the contention doesn't hold up. When the rate of increase of available handguns was at its highest (1980), teenage suicide had already leveled off, and even *decreased* from 1977. And while teenage suicides have remained constant for 15 years in the U.S., teens in Europe are killing themselves at a rapidly rising pace, even though gun control is much stricter there.

Senators John Chafee and Joseph Biden have testified officially before the Senate Judiciary Committee that 135,000 kids take guns to school every day. The American Bar Association and *USA Today* repeat the claim. Senator Christopher Dodd raised the number to 186,000. They are all guilty of perpetuating a distorted interpretation of an actual study conducted by the Centers for Disease Control.

The 1991 survey asked students if they had carried a gun for protection in the last 30 days. The calculated total of 135,000 might have resulted from an assumption that every child who said he or she had carried a gun *anywhere even once* in 30 days, must have carried it *to school every day.* This was not the focus of the study, although many anti-gunners have construed it to be. The report itself explained, "Students were not asked if they car-

---

[32] *Vital Statistics of the United States,* "Mortality: Part A," National Center for Health Statistics, U.S. Public Health Service, Washington, DC, 1991, vol. II..

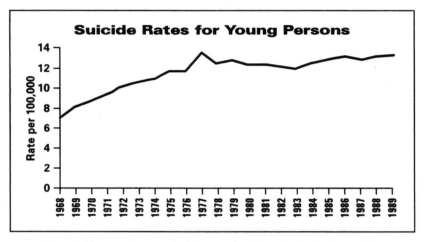

The suicide rate for young persons rose sharply in the late 1960s through the mid-1970s, and has remained stable since then.

ried weapons onto school grounds." Many of the students clearly carried their guns in their vehicles for protection at night, but never took them to school. Florida State University criminologist Gary Kleck says from 16,000 to 17,000 students carry guns to school on any given day—that's about 1 in 800, or 12 percent of the alarmists' claim of 135,000—and mostly for self-protection.

It is a sad social commentary when the fiber of society is so threadbare that kids feel the need to protect themselves with guns at school, but removing guns from law-abiding citizens is not going to fix the problem. Teenagers are more likely to be the victims of violent crime than any other age group in America. In 1986, one out of every six teenagers was the victim of a street crime, compared to one in nine adults, and youths are twice as likely to be assaulted, robbed, or raped as are adults.[33] In a six-month period in 1988-89, more than 400,000 students were victims of violent crimes at school.[34]

A Brooklyn public school superintendent told the New York *Daily News*, "A lot of parents ...give their children weapons to protect themselves when they leave the tenements." And a student wrote the *Washington Post*, December 1, 1988:

> ... I think students bring weapons to school to save their own lives. They have a constant fear of being attacked .... To the outsider, this ... may seem all blown out of proportion, or just a plain lie. The truth is there are drugs in the schools. There are kids robbing other kids of their money and personal belongings. And these kids who are com-

---

[33] *School Safety*, "Kids and Crime," James R. Weasel, Spring 1988, pp. 4-5.

[34] *Teenage Victims: A National Crime Survey Report*, Bureau of Justice Statistics, Catherine J. Whitaker & Lisa Bastican, U.S. Department of Justice, Washington, DC, May 1991, NCJ-128129.

mitting the crimes also carry weapons such as knives and handguns and they are not afraid to use them.

There's no doubt that we have a serious problem on our hands. I just hope we can find some way to solve it.

The problem is not with the 90 percent of 16,000-plus kids who carry guns for self-protection; the problem is with the ten percent of armed students who are committing crimes at school. (Only 1,700 gun-related crimes were committed in American schools in 1986).[35] And, as with any other sector of the populace, when the law-abiding majority are disarmed by restrictive laws and regulations, only the minority criminal element will benefit.

It's unnerving that a single student in the United States of America should feel the need to go to school armed. Further, any crime committed with a gun at school is appalling. But removing guns will not stop crime at schools. In 1986, 41,500 aggravated assaults occurred in American schools, as did 44,000 robberies. Remember, only 1,700 of these crimes involved the use of guns. Is anyone so foolish as to believe the 83,800 assaults and robberies committed *without* guns somehow would not have happened if guns were removed from the equation?

Naming guns as the ultimate villain is an easy way to avoid dealing with the larger picture—a violent society spawning violent youth. To focus on this single instrument of violence is a deliberate way to inspire emotional "knee-jerk" gun control legislation while doing nothing to address the causes of violence.

A team of renowned researchers wrote in the *American Journal of Diseases of Children*:

---

[35] *School Safety*, Spring 1988, p. 4.

> It is clear that the problem of violence in inner city schools cannot be isolated from the problems of violence in larger society; violent neighborhoods and violent communities will produce violent schools, whatever measures the schools themselves adopt. It is equally clear that this 'larger' problem will not yield to simplistic, unicausal solutions. In this connection, it is useful to point out that everything that leads to gun-related violence is already against the law. What is needed are not new and more restrictive gun laws but rather a concerted effort to rebuild the social structure of inner cities.[36]

The solution to the problem is not to disarm the victims who are trying to protect themselves. Action must be taken instead against the criminal element threatening the students, and against the societal conditions that breed the element. Meanwhile, law-abiding citizens must not be disarmed, or made into criminals for exercising their constitution right to self-protection—*no matter their age*. Is a teenager targeted for gang rape or assault any less entitled to effective self-defense than a woman or man of 40 or 50 years? Most armed students are coping with a rotten societal environment.

The breakdown of American moral fiber is highly concentrated in the inner cities. Gun prohibition advocates would have the general citizenry believe anything else in order to promote their agenda. Strategies are employed from exaggerating gun accident statistics to announcing epidemics of suicide. A common and effective tactic is to instill fear of gun crime—especially homicides. For instance, *Fortune* magazine has warned its affluent readership the "... onslaught of childhood violence

---

[36] *American Journal of Diseases of Children*, Dr. Joseph Sheley, p. 682.

knows no boundaries of race, geography, or class."[37] And the *Journal of the American Medical Association* insists, "It's not limited to the inner city."[38]

The Columbine High School shooting and all of the other killings at the hands of maniacal misfits are the most grievous and unimaginable tragedies. Even more deplorable are those politicians who exploit these tragedies for their own selfish, political gain. None of these "honorable" leaders has proposed any solutions that would have prevented even one bullet from being fired at any of these school disasters. Furthermore, and most importantly, none of these political gun control proposals coincide with fundamental principles as espoused by the founders of our once-sacred Constitution.

Perhaps the most profound and prophetic statement ever made by President Ronald Reagan best describes our political floundering in response to youth violence when he said, "Government is not the solution to our problems, government is the problem."

Graphs provided by the U.S. Department of Justice and researcher David Kopel (next page) compare youth homicides by age, race and gender, as well as geographical setting. Kopel says the intent is not to negate concern about the youth homicide problem, but to focus on causes—like governmental and societal racism—that set a moral obligation for all Americans to respond to the crisis in the context that it exists.

---

[37] *Fortune*, "Kids Are Killing, Dying, Bleeding," Ronald Henkoff, August 10, 1992.

[38] *Journal of the American Medical Association*, "Gun-Associated Violence Increasingly Viewed as Public Health Challenge," Paul Cotton, 1992, pp. 1171-1174.

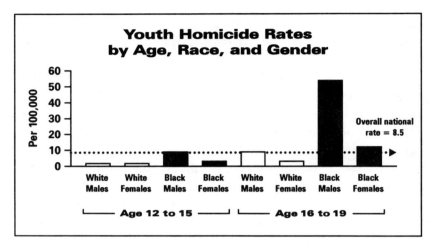

The homicide rate for most groups of teenagers is low, but the rate
for black males aged 16 to 19 years is enormous.

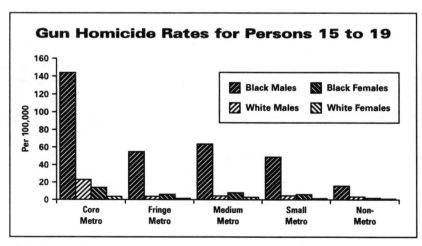

The crisis of black teenage male homicide is particularly acute in heavily
urbanized areas, where legal restrictions on guns are already greatest.

It's important to note that most major American cities saw a leveling off of homicide rates in 1992.[39] Also, it should be taken into account that from seven to 13 percent of American firearms "homicides" occur as legitimate defenses against violent criminal attack.[40]

While no one can deny there's a homicide problem within the American society, the issue cannot be addressed effectively without a realistic understanding of it. To say homicides are rampant everywhere, equally spread among all ethnicities, income brackets, geographical settings and education levels is to further diminish the truth and any chance of dealing with the problem.

The crisis of America's rising teenage murder rate is directly linked to the much larger social crisis in our educational system and in the nation's inner cities. Until the bases for social decay, lack of parental involvement and the destruction of the American family are addressed *and modified*, the murder crisis will continue.

The assertion that the availability of guns is relative to the frequency of homicides doesn't stack up very high. In fact, just the opposite appears to be true. Regions where gun ownership is high typically have lower homicide rates. Also, while whites across the country have a far higher rate of gun ownership than blacks, they have a much lower homicide rate.[41] And a verifiable *inverse* correlation exists between periods of high gun ownership

---

[39] *Gun Control Digest*, "Homicide Down, Leveling Off in Many Major Cities," quote by Criminal Justice professor William Wilbanks, December 14, 1992, pp. 9-10.

[40] *Point Blank*, Gary Kleck.

[41] *Point Blank*, Gary Kleck.

and low homicide rates, as with periods of low gun ownership with high homicide rates.[42]

David Kopel (in his *Children and Guns* report) suggested that low American homicide rates in areas where gun ownership is often high should cause theorists to think again about gun prohibition as a viable response to rising murder rates. Professor Hans Toch, of the State University of New York's School of Criminology, studied the causes and cures of American violence for the Eisenhower Administration. In the late 1960s, Toch believed that "reducing the availability of the handgun *will* reduce firearms violence." (Emphasis from source) However, based on more recent research, Toch has found:

> ... when used for protection, firearms can seriously inhibit aggression and can provide a psychological buffer against the fear of crime. Furthermore, the fact that national patterns show little violent crime where guns are most dense implies that guns do not elicit aggression in any meaningful way. Quite the contrary, these findings suggest that high saturations of guns in places, or something correlated with that condition, inhibit illegal aggression.[43]

Just as the availability of guns apparently has little to do with the frequency of homicide, neither do stringent gun laws. Scotland, for example, has rigorous gun control laws and a homicide rate for young males (15-24) three times higher than

---

[42] *Shooting Industry*, "Firearm Production, Imports, and Exports," Walter J. Howe, January 1992, pp. 91-118.

[43] *Psychology and Social Advocacy*, eds. P. Suefeld & P. Tetlock, "Research & Policy: The Case of Gun Control," Toch & Lizotte, Hemisphere Press, New York, NY, 1990.

Switzerland—where the government issues a fully automatic Sig-Sauer assault rifle to every adult male and trains him to use it.[44]

At the risk of belaboring a point, gun control laws are not going to stop teenagers from possessing guns, or from shooting one another with guns. Neither can the point be made too often that as long as the debate over social decay in America focuses only on symptoms—guns, gangs, drugs—there will never be a solution to the problem. Yephet Copeland, a former member of the Hoover Street Crips in Los Angeles, says, "We need better schools and jobs. That's the way you stop the killing. You have to offer hope. If there's no hope, the killing will go on—gun ban or not."[45]

Florida State University criminologist Gary Kleck writes:

> Fixating on guns seems to be, for many people, a fetish which allows them to ignore intransigent causes of American violence, including its dying cities, inequality, deteriorating family structure, and the all-pervasive economic and social consequences of a history of slavery and racism .... All parties to the crime debate would do well to give more concentrated attention to more difficult, but far more relevant, issues like how to generate more good-paying jobs for the underclass, an issue which is at the heart of the violence problem.[46]

---

[44] *The Samurai, the Mountie, and the Cowboy: Should America Adopt the Gun Controls of Other Democracies?*, David Kopel, Prometheus Books, Buffalo, NY, 1992.

[45] *Los Angeles Times*, January 18, 1993.

[46] "Guns and Violence: A Summary of the Field," Gary Kleck, a paper presented at the Annual Meeting of the American Political Science Association, August 29, 1991, p. 18.

Listen to the voices:

"... national patterns show little violent crime where guns are most dense."
—Professor Hans Toch

"If there's no hope, the killing will go on—gun ban or not."
—former Crip Yephet Copeland

"Fixating on guns seems to be ... a fetish which allows them to ignore the more intransigent causes of American violence ..."
—criminologist Gary Kleck

From the bloody inner-city streets to the cavernous halls of academia, they're saying the same thing. Guns are not the problem. You don't treat AIDS with an aspirin. Neither can you prop up a crumbling society by chiseling away at the foundation of a nation. Further, "feel good" laws achieve only superficial (and largely negative) effects. There are 200,000,000 guns in the United States—most of them in the hands of responsible citizens—as provided by the constitutional right to "*keep and bear Arms*."

If the U.S. Constitution becomes further impaired by politicians bent on disarming an honest citizenry, then the United States of America will have become a far more dangerous place to live—not only by threat of the criminal element, but even more so by the *political* element.

The issue of kids and guns is not all that different than the issue of adults and guns. Some kids are criminals. Some kids feel the need to protect themselves. Kids carry guns. Kids shoot people with guns. Gun prohibitionists, liberal politicians and the media sensationalize the issue more with kids than adults because it helps pass illegal legislation and improves ratings.

Guns have nothing to do with the psychological conditioning that turns innocent babies into emotionless killers in the few short years of their childhoods. Society does. A voice from the street—William Fox, a former Brawling Street Crip—says, "It's not the guns that have to change. It's the people that have to change."[47]

Choking off the liberties of law-abiding Americans will not change anyone for the better.

---

[47] *Los Angeles Times*, January 18, 1993.

I ask, sir, what is the militia? It is the whole people, except for a few public officials ... . To disarm the people is the best and most effectual way to enslave them.

—George Mason

Facts with Faces

It was a beautiful autumn day—sun shining, the air fresh and alive—the kind of day that makes living in Texas a blessing. Dr. Suzie Gratia was going to lunch with her parents, Al and Ursula Gratia, who had celebrated their 47th wedding anniversary only a couple of weeks earlier.

Dr. Gratia is a chiropractor. She has worked hard, building a respectable business in Killeen. She's petite and attractive, friendly and professional. Growing up in the Southwest, she had been exposed to guns and had learned how to use them. She has no interest in the "sporting" value of firearms because she detests hunting, and always has.

Suzie received a pistol as a gift from a friend when she was 21 years old. She kept it with her most of the time. At age 27, Suzie obtained another gun—a Smith & Wesson airweight, snub-nosed five-shot .38. It fit perfectly inside her purse. She carried it with her everywhere—*concealed*. Dr. Gratia—not a street criminal, but an educated and responsible businesswoman—made a decision to disobey a Texas law making it a felony to carry a concealed weapon into certain public establishments.

To Dr. Gratia, keeping a gun was a kind of insurance policy. It felt good knowing it was nearby—just in case. She her right to self-protection as God-given, and more important than obeying a law clearly in violation of the U.S. Constitution.

Then Dr. Gratia made a mistake in judgment—one she'll regret forever. Under Texas law, restaurants are "public establishments" where concealed weapons are forbidden. A felony conviction would cost her her chiropractor's license, her reputation and her livelihood. Having grown increasingly fearful of her own government, and of being found with a gun in her purse, Suzie decided to leave the gun in her car. After nearly ten years of feeling secure in knowing she was armed and capable of protecting herself, she stepped into the parking lot a few ounces lighter—and a lot more vulnerable.

It was October 16, 1991. Dr. Gratia walked with her parents into Luby's Cafeteria. It was just past noon. The restaurant was filled with customers. The Gratias were not able to sit at their usual table. They had just placed their order when the world stopped spinning.

A pickup truck came crashing through the wall and windows, running over customers as they ate. Patrons screamed and cried, frozen with confusion and fear. From inside the vehicle, the driver began firing a pistol into the panic-stricken crowd. The madman climbed out of the pickup, continuing to fire, striking several patrons as they scrambled for cover.

Dr. Gratia and her father tipped over their table and pulled Mrs. Gratia down behind it. Suzie's first impulse was to help those injured and crying, but she did not want to attract attention to her parents behind the table. The gunman continued firing at anything that moved. He stood but 15 feet away, his back turned, as he carried out the methodical slaughter of restaurant patrons. Instinctively, Dr. Gratia opened her purse and grabbed for her gun. Her heart sank. *IT'S IN THE CAR!* she realized. She watched helplessly as the man kept shooting.

Frustrated and desperate, Al Gratia charged the gunman. At the last instant, the shooter turned and fired into Mr. Gratia's chest. Suzie saw the wound and knew her father would die.

Dr. Gratia thought now only of her mother and getting her out alive. She saw an open window as their only chance. She tugged her mother's arm and told her to follow. Suzie jumped out and turned to help her mother through, but Ursula Gratia had gone to her dying husband instead. The woman held her life's companion in her arms as the killer approached. Suzie saw the eyes of her mother and the gunman meet, then Mrs. Gratia dropped her gaze and waited. The killer shot her once in the head.[48]

Ursula Gratia was the last victim shot. Police fired into the room, slightly wounding the gunman. He then ran to a back room and shot himself to death. Twenty-three people, including Al and Ursula Gratia, lay dead about the restaurant. Only a handful of victims survived their wounds.

Dr. Suzie Gratia walked away from the massacre unhurt, but she lives daily with feelings of guilt, frustration and anger. Her guilt is expressed as self-criticism for not having done more to save her mother. Her frustration comes from knowing she removed her gun from her purse after having it there most of her adult life. And her anger is aimed directly at the lawmakers who violated her rights to self-protection. Suzie Gratia feels betrayed and forsaken by "public servants" sworn in the name of Deity to "protect and defend" her rights.

---

[48] The entire incident, as shared by Suzie Gratia with Sheriff Richard Mack on KFYI Radio, Phoenix, AZ, July 21, 1994.

Dr. Gratia finds it paradoxical that a "law" designed to protect honest citizens should, in effect, get them killed—that a "law" should render an entire restaurant full of citizens completely defenseless against the whims of a psychotic madman. Wherein lies the greater crime—the madman destroying innocent lives or the trusted constitutional guard tending more to politics and reelection than to the God-given rights of Americans?

How many lives could Dr. Gratia have saved on that dreadful autumn afternoon? Anti-gunners argue that disarming the public is justified if "a single life can be saved." Conversely, gun rights advocates might adopt the same rationale—that if "a single life can be saved," then every private citizen should be armed. At least 23 people at Luby's Cafeteria on that fateful day in 1991 would probably agree—if they could. Instead, 23 people gave their lives in the name of an unconstitutional law. This typifies the result of most restrictive gun control laws—the criminals remain armed and become more indiscriminate in their deeds because they have no fear of an unarmed public.

The Founding Fathers provided the perfect method for discouraging thieves, pillagers and murderers ("... *the right to keep and bear Arms* ..."). Modern legislators seem determined to promote the opposite effect. Criminals have never had so much unchallenged freedom, and honest citizens have never been so vulnerable as they are today.

Some citizens are not rolling over for the anti-gunners. A burglar in Tulsa, Oklahoma, found that out on July 20, 1994. Armed with a pocket knife and 15-inch screwdriver, the unidentified intruder broke into a home where a 13-year-old boy was watching after his three siblings, ages 12, nine and seven. The children hid in their parents' bedroom. When the intruder tried to break down the door, the oldest child fired his father's .357

Magnum through the door of the bedroom. Mortally wounded, the burglar staggered outside and collapsed. (Names are withheld in deference to the family.)

Tulsa Police Sergeant Steve Emmons said, "They were doing what they had been taught to do. The parents had taken the time to give their children some instruction."[49]

Four youngsters were kept safe (and alive) because a Tulsa family believed in their right to keep and bear arms. Many politicians and anti-gun groups would see that right taken away. Moving *too* fast in that direction would spark widespread opposition from the American heartland, so clever political strategists have chosen to go for it a little at a time. But their actions are becoming more grandiose. Banning "assault weapons," proposals to ban *all* firearms, even a plan to abolish the Second Amendment, illustrate their growing sense of smug confidence.

Honesty is on the side of gun owners. Deceit and trickery are tools of the abolitionists. The U.S. Constitution was written to protect honest Americans. Attempts to dilute its content and meaning must be met with fierce resistance in the polling places of America, in the halls of Congress—and, if necessary, in the streets, the hills and dales of the Republic.

---

[49] Associated Press, July 21, 1994.

Firearms stand next in importance to the Constitution itself. They are the American people's liberty teeth and keystone under independence. To secure peace, security and happiness, the rifle and the pistol are equally indispensable. The very atmosphere of firearms everywhere restrains evil interference—they deserve a place of honor with all that is good.

—George Washington

The HCI Lie

Handgun Control, Inc. (HCI) is not a friend of law-abiding Americans. Neither is this handgun-abolitionist group a friend of the U.S. Constitution and Bill of Rights. HCI has emerged as a strong anti-gun lobbying voice, with spokeswoman Sarah Brady often eliciting sympathetic support by speaking from beside her disabled husband's wheelchair. Their most touted accomplishment was congressional passage of the so-called Brady Handgun Law.

But like any other group dedicated to altering the basic structure of America, HCI must develop stratagems. Sarah Brady cannot possibly believe when all honest Americans are disarmed, then armed criminals will cease to prey upon them. But her husband was struck down by a crazy man's bullet. Her life, at that moment, was irrevocably changed. Her mission now is to somehow compensate for Jim Brady's tragic circumstance by taking handguns away from all honest citizens. The mission cannot be accomplished legally under the Constitution as written by the Founding Fathers. Therefore, more subversive tactics are employed. The following pages contain part of an HCI draft plan (disavowed by HCI when leaked), presented as written:

HCI – Confidential Document
DO NOT DISTRIBUTE/NOT FOR GENERAL CIRCULATION

Attachment 1:

Stamped Received   Stamped CONFIDENTIAL
Signed 1/6/94

Confidential Information for use by Lobbyists or Senior Officers ONLY!

I. Proposed License Fees – 1994-1995 Gun Control Proposals

Fees based on calculated costs of records maintenance, centralized computer system set up, cost of new computer and record keeping equipment, administrative costs of new federal and state offices, cost of enforcement and inspection, and calculated cost of gun violence to society.

These listings and the documentation used to calculate these suggested fee schedules will be made available to Federal Law Enforcement Authorities and the U.S. Dept. of the Treasury for review, when the time is right. Additional material will be made available to key politicians when proposing any fee related legislation. These suggestions will be instrumental in determining the nature of future gun control legislation and proposals.

THE FOLLOWING INFORMATION IS CONFIDENTIAL!! DO NOT DISTRIBUTE BEYOND THE OFFICES OF HCI UNLESS HAND DELIVERED TO AN APPROVED STATE OR FEDERAL LEGISLATOR OR LAW ENFORCEMENT OFFICIAL.

a) Handgun License Fees:

Year 1 to 2:
Program can begin at a relatively low cost to discourage non-compliance:
  Suggested Fee Schedule: $50 - $75 annual fee

Year 3 to 4:
Fees would be raised to reflect the cost of enforcement and discourage new ownership:

Suggested Fee Schedule: $150 - $250 annual fee

Year 5 to 8:
If private ownership has not been prohibited by this time then fees can be gradually increased to discourage private ownership:
Suggested Fee Schedule: $550 - $625 annual fee

b) Suggested penalties for non-compliance with licensing:
(Penalties would have to be formally outlined by state and federal lawmakers)
    (a) Failure to acquire license
      $1,000 / 6 mos. in jail and revocation of ability to own firearms
    (b) Failure to maintain license
      $5,000 / 12 mos. in jail and revocation of ability to own firearms
    (c) Failure to turn over guns for destruction after lapse of license
      $15,000 / 18 mos. in jail and revocation of ability to own firearms

Failure to re-new license or notify issuing authority of change of status would be considered a felony. All firearms own [sic] would be then considered contraband and could then be confiscated. State or local law enforcement authorities would be prohibited from retaining or re-selling any confiscated firearm. A record of destruction would have to be issued via common carrier to the federal government not later than 60 days after confiscation.

c) Rifle & Shotgun License:
Program can begin at $30 or at a cost determined to maintain federal records on ownership and registration.
Suggested Fee Schedule: $30 - $148 annual fee

d) State Licensing of Firearms:
The states can collect revenue by initiating state license requirements. The Dept. of Justice for each state will be responsible for initiating the programs at state level. The licensing fees would be relatively equal with the federal fee requirements.
Suggested Fee schedule: $74 - $150 annual fee

e) Local Licensing of Firearms:
The U.S. Treasury Dept. should look into any legal precedent which will allow the federal authorities to allow cities and towns to restrict ownership or initiate licensing requirements, with the cost of each annual license to reflect the cost of records maintenance and enforcement.
   Suggested Fee schedule: $48 - $113 annual fee

f) Arsenal License: (currently at 20 guns or 1,000 rds. of ammo)
   Suggested Fee schedule: $300 - $1,000 annual fee
   Alternate Yearly Fee Schedule:
      If guns owned exceed 20 - $200 per gun over the limit
      If ammo qty. exceeds 1000 - $100 per each 50 rounds over the limit
   (Fees are flexible due to requirements of local law enforcement)

g) Suggested Penalty for Non-Compliance of Arsenal Licensing Law:
$5,000 / 8 mos in jail, confiscation of all firearms related property and the revocation of ability to own firearms. (Final Disposition would have to be determined by the Dept. of Justice and the state and federal legislatures)

h) Safe License:
   Suggested fee schedule: $228 - $392 annual fee
(Fees based on calculations of set up of computerized records keeping system, enforcement and registration processing)

i) Ammunition Registration & License:
   Suggested Fee schedule: $55 - $117 fee for license to buy ammunition
(Fees based on calculations of set up of computerized records keeping system, enforcement and registration processing)

j) Federal license for Re-loading (or possession of re-loading equipment)
   Suggested fee schedule: $130 - $175 annual fee

k) Ammunition Safe License Fee:
   Suggested Fee schedule: $55 - $75 annual fee

l) Range license (New Federal License on target, outdoor/indoor ranges)
   Suggested Fee schedule: $12,100 - $15,500 annual fee

m) Range Tax Fee (imposed on Federally licensed gun ranges)
Suggested Fee schedule: $85 - $100 collected per person, per visit

n) Inspection License: (Verifying the records of guns and storage)
This would defray the cost of inspection of firearms safes in businesses or private homes)
Suggested Fee schedule: $588 - $678 annual fee

II. <u>Suggestions which can be made immediately available to Key Politicians and the Secretary of the U.S. Treasury:</u>

a) Increase Dealers License (Federal Firearms License 01 and 02):
Suggested Fee schedule: $600 - $750 annual fee

b) Increased Title 1 Manufacturing Fees:
Suggested Fee schedule: $6,200 - $9,400 annual fee

c) Increased Title 2 Manufacturing Fees:
Suggested Fee schedule: $13,405 - $18,210 annual fee

III. <u>An Estimate of the fiscal impact of the licensing of firearms ownership:</u>

	Worst Case:	Best Case:
Federal Handgun License:	$50	$625
Federal Rifle & Shotgun License:	$30	$148
State Gun License Fee:	$74	$150
Local Gun License Fee:	$48	$113
Arsenal License Fee:	$300	$1,000
Safe License Fee:	$228	$392
Ammunition License Fee:	$55	$117
Re-Loading License Fee:	$130	$175
Ammo Safe License Fee:	$55	$75
Ammo Inspection Fee:	$588	$678
Total Annual Cost:	$1,558	$3,473

This cost is not unreasonable, since it would offset considerably the estimated $60 billion dollars in medical and social costs related to gun violence. If a gun enthusiast feels he needs such firepower, it is not unreasonable to require him to provide the money necessary to offset the cost to society of such firepower. Ultimately such action would take the glamour and attraction out of firearms ownership and decrease the numbers of gun owners in the U.S. to a manageable number.

IV. Reduction of Gun Owner Population and Potential Yearly Revenue

The federal government estimates that around 65-75 million Americans own guns. These fees and the licensing requirements would allow us to take guns out of the hands of an estimated 30 million unsuitable or ineligible individuals. The fees for the remaining qualifying individuals would additionally reduce the number to about 14 million gun owners. The estimated federal and state revenues from such fee schedules would constitute a minimum of $21.812 billion dollars (Worst Case) to an estimated $48.622 billion (Best Case) annually. Our eventual goal is to reduce the number of licensees to zero. The revenue itself can be utilized to achieve this goal. ...

AND THE CRIMINALS WILL STILL HAVE GUNS!!!
        This HCI document continues its conspiratorial tone and plan for yet a couple of more pages. It's purpose is not to address the issue of crime in the streets; it is to disarm honest citizens. Let's go back and look at some key elements of the plan, which, in turn, reflect the ideology behind it.

        "... begin at a relatively low cost to discourage non-compliance:"

---

[50] HCI–Confidential Document, January 6, 1994, pp. 1-3.

This, coupled with extreme penalties for non-compliance, is but a design to locate all the guns owned by the general American public.

"If private ownership has not been prohibited ..."
The ultimate goal.

"... fees can be gradually increased to discourage private ownership:"
A plan to legally disarm America without touching the Second Amendment.

"Failure to re-new license ... would be considered a felony."
Remember, there are 200,000,000 guns in the United States, most of them in the hands of about 70,000,000 God-fearing, law-abiding, freedom-loving Americans. Now we have a way to turn many of them into felons, who cannot legally own firearms.

"All firearms ... could then be confiscated."
All they need is an excuse like this to circumvent Fourth Amendment protection from unreasonable searches and seizures.

All of the "suggested fee schedules" for licensing are strictly punitive. Millions of Americans, who are safer for having a handgun, rifle or shotgun in their homes, would not be able to afford these exorbitant *annual* fees, thus being forced to give up their guns—and their constitutional right to keep and bear arms. It's ironic, too, that HCI would prefer to see accredited shooting ranges forced to close and responsible target shooters prohibited from practice by unrealistic fees; street criminals do not hone up their skills at the municipal range. And it's ludicrous that gun owners should be forced to buy an annual $600 Inspection License that would give permission for federal searches of the gun owners' offices and private homes. Gun owners, in effect, would be paying the government to violate their Second and Fourth Amendment rights!

"... $60 billion dollars in medical and social costs related to gun violence."

This is a surrogate issue intended to lend credibility to their argument. Automobile owners are not paying excessive license fees to cover the "medical and social costs" related to traffic deaths and injuries.

"... take the glamour and attraction out of firearms ownership ..."

Most gun owners don't feel there is glamour or attraction tied to gun ownership; they own guns for protection of themselves and their property, or for hunting. Gun "collectors," on the other hand, *do* feel an affection for these instruments of precision and beauty—much the same as "collectors" of antiques, stamps or butterflies. Seventy million gun owners in the United States are simply not walking around with "such firepower" protruding from every pocket, looking for an opportunity to use it.

"... decrease the numbers of gun owners in the U.S. to a manageable number."

Manageable by whom? Local police? BATF agents? United Nations' troops?

Wake up, America! Don't you find this a little frightening? Do you think it can't happen in the United States?

Handgun Control, Inc., activists have a powerful voice in Washington. Federal lawmakers listen to their demands. In their own words, the above plan "would allow us to take guns out of the hands of an estimated 30 million unsuitable or ineligible individuals." What determines "unsuitable or ineligible"—an inability to pay? And who is "us"? How involved does HCI intend to be with taking guns "out of the hands" of "30 million" citizens? They proudly proclaim *"our* goal is to reduce the number of licensees to zero."

They can only do this with the help of Congress—and they have it. In 1993-94, Senators Moynihan, Metzenbaum, Chafee, DeConcini and Bradley, as well as Congressmen Gutierrez, Schumer, Stark, Gibbons, Mfume, Hughes, Owens and Reynolds, all sponsored legislation aimed at banning handguns, shotguns, rifles and ammunition. The Clinton Administration of the 1990s strongly favored gun control as a necessary cog on the wheel moving our free nation toward a system of Central World Government.

The Federal Government already has the mechanisms in place to "put down" any armed "insurrection" of American gun owners banded together in defense of their constitutional rights. When a president of Bill Clinton's socialistic persuasion sees a *"well regulated Militia"* of armed Americans rising up against his achievements, all he needs then to do is declare a national state of emergency.

During a declared national emergency, Executive Orders— already recorded in the *Federal Register* and treated by Congress as the "law of the land"—can be ordered (by the President) into effect at any time. A sampling of Executive Orders meant to apply under this condition include:

Order No. 10995: All communications media seized by the Federal Government.

Order No. 10997: Seizure of all electrical power, fuels, including gasoline and minerals.

Order No. 10998: Seizure of all food resources, farms and farm equipment.

Order No. 10999: Seizure of all kinds of transportation, including personal cars, and control of all highways and seaports.

Order No. 11000: Seizure of all civilians for work under Federal Government supervision.

Order No. 11001: Federal takeover of all health, education and welfare.

Order No. 11002: Postmaster General empowered to register every man, woman and child in the U.S.A.

Order No. 11003: Seizure of all aircraft and airports by the Federal Government.

Order No. 11004: Housing and Finance authority may shift population from one locality to another.

Order No. 11005: Seizure of railroads, inland waterways, and storage facilities.

Order No. 11490: Combines most of the above and adds the authority to regulate the amount of personal money that may be withdrawn from banks, or savings and loan institutions.[51]

(Please read the list again.)

---

[51] *The Federal Register.*

By implementing Executive Order No. 11490, the President of the United States could effectively place the entire nation under martial law, and would serve, then, as the head of a military dictatorship.

OUR FEDERAL GOVERNMENT WAS NEVER INTENDED TO HAVE THIS MUCH POWER!

U.S. Marines are being carefully conditioned to join forces with United Nations' troops when the time comes to face off against Americans and confiscate all privately owned guns. At such time as that should happen, the principles of freedom supported by the United States Constitution and Bill of Rights— ownership of property, freedoms of speech, press and religion, rights to privacy and choice—will all cease to exist.

"Free" Americans are going to have to decide how much loss of freedom through government control they are willing to tolerate, and they must decide while they are still free. We have become a nation of sheep, doing whatever the Federal Government tells us to do. Odds favor a frightening continuation of that trend. On the opposite end of the spectrum, a far-flung contingent vows an armed resistance to the final erosion of rights.

The strongest potential for preservation of American freedom and constitutional rights, however, exists on middle ground. Between passivism and civil war are awareness, education and the political battlefield. The many millions of silent Americans who *know* the U.S. Constitution is a good and workable document must be made *aware* of the many hammers and chisels poised to knock it down. Every free citizen must begin to question the love affair between New Age politicians, left-wing special interests, and mainstream national media. Why are scandals being ignored? Why are social conditions in our own inner cities less important than social issues in Third World nations around the globe? How do politicians making $140,000 a year come home millionaires? Why is a socialistic president a hero to the media? Why is the U.S. Constitution used in court more frequently to protect detractors (pornographers, traitors and criminals) than law-abiding citizens? Everyone must take an interest, get involved, get educated, and help to spread the truth.

Finally, *vote the conscience of America!* Freedom-loving Americans are still by far the majority. When a senator introduces unconstitutional legislation, he should be out of a job. When a congressman accepts gifts from special-interest groups, he should be out of a job. When a president offers control of American troops and property to the United Nations, he should be out of a job. The American public has that power and ability.

Ignorance is a cancer. Laziness is a sin. Complacency will destroy the nation we live in.

The only difference between today's slavery and the slavery of the old South is that at least the plantation owners paid for the chains.

—Alan Keyes, presidential candidate

From My Cold Dead Fingers

... Arms discourage and keep the invader and plunderer in awe, and preserve order in the world as well as property. ... Horrid mischief would ensue were the law-abiding deprived of the use of them.

—Thomas Paine, 1775

Activism or Passivism

While every course of action may not be a totally correct one, someone doing something is better than everyone doing nothing. There are several small movements afloat to turn the current stampede from the looming black abyss. Some concerned groups and individuals simply put forth ideas for others to act upon. From either source, there is hope and encouragement.

The Independence Institute at Golden, Colorado, is a think tank. Its directors and members participate in nonpartisan studies and issue in-depth analyses based on extensive collections of data. Because children and guns are so inextricably tied together in many minds, David Kopel compiled an "Issue Paper" for the Institute dealing exclusively with the topic from that perspective. After dispelling a great many myths, Kopel made some surprising and sensible suggestions.

He said truancy laws at schools are archaic—that forcing students who do not want to learn to be present on school premises only breeds rebellion, and disrupts students who do want to learn. He said schools should not be modeled after prisons. Also, poor people should be able to choose the schools their children attend, rather than being forced to attend dysfunctional and dangerous public schools in the inner cities where more affluent parents would never dream of sending their children. Kopel says violence is virtually nonexistent in inner-city parochial and private schools.[52]

Other suggestions from Kopel include a better juvenile court system, where judges have time to learn about their cases, and open court records, where the offenses of juveniles are not hidden from the courts when those juveniles commit criminal acts after the age of majority. Juvenile offenders should be forced to pay restitution, and should *know* they will be punished for their misdeeds.[53]

Kopel also believes kids should be taught about and familiarized with guns by their parents, and not their peers. He thinks the media and entertainment industries glamorize violence and minimize the value of life. And he says politically slanted classroom education about firearms is totally inappropriate, and even destructive.[54]

Finally, Kopel says government must begin dealing with social pathologies. He says it's foolish to pretend that gun control will work where drug control has failed. In the long run, he adds, the most effective solutions will be found in addressing the social conditions that have caused so many inner-city youth to value their own lives and the lives of others so cheaply.

Kopel writes: "There are no simple solutions to today's social pathologies; if there were, the solutions would already have been implemented. Yet the sooner it is recognized that political discussion about violence must start debating the ways to remedy urban decay, and must abandon the focus on useless gestures

---

[52] *Children and Guns: Sensible Solutions*, David B. Kopel, p. 35.

[53] *Children and Guns: Sensible Solutions*, Kopel, p. 50.

[54] *Children and Guns: Sensible Solutions*, Kopel, pp. 51, 56, 59.

such as gun control, the sooner America will begin making forward progress."[55]

Contemporary government is attempting to force all of us to live within restricted cocoons of behavior. They want to eliminate crime, hunger, poverty, pain and, most of all, choice!

However, as long as the human race remains imperfect there will be violence, suicide, accidents and murder. Psychogenic disorders, anger, jealousy, greed, competition, addiction, desperation, despondency and most chronic social ills affecting teenagers also affect adults. Statistics and incidents involving teens typically evoke more emotion. But the decay of social and moral values is not unique to particular age groups. To begin the healing process, government (and society) must look beyond the symptoms of the condition. Banning guns will do no more to reduce crime and violence than banning drugs did to decrease crime, addiction, AIDS and overdoses.

Not everyone in Washington believes you can fix a cancer with a Band-Aid. Congressman Roscoe G. Bartlett of Maryland introduced the Citizens' Self-Defense Act of 1993, calling for the "... right to obtain firearms for security, and to use firearms in defense of self, family, or home, and to provide for the enforcement of such right."[56] In a letter to constituents, Bartlett said the bill would put an end to gun control laws that target law-abiding citizens instead of criminals. His effort was noble and noteworthy. And while H.R.1276 may not have made it to a full House vote, it at least demonstrated one legislator's conviction that law-abiding Americans have the right to protect themselves. Bartlett simply supports the Second Amendment. He's disturbed

---

[55] *Children and Guns: Sensible Solutions*, Kopel, pp. 64-65.
[56] H.R.1276, March 10, 1993.

that lawmakers have exceeded their authority to the point that legislation such as his is even needed.

American citizens should be disturbed that Bartlett's bill did not become law. Preservation of the Constitution is not a priority to some other members of Congress. (*They should find themselves out of a job!*) Only a loud and persistent voice from American voters will get their attention. The Republic of the United States is still a government "of the people, by the people and for the people." The people have the vote—the people have the power. For too long, Washington politicians and bureaucrats have believed *they* have the power. It's time to send them a message. A tidal wave of grassroots American sentiment, an unprecedented turnout of dissatisfied voters at the polls, the hiring of more conservative politicians, will send that message. The citizens of the several states can reinstate themselves to power in a single movement.

Organized movements range from those strong on good intentions and soft on action to others bordering on radical. Somewhere within that spectrum lies the Gun Owners of America, dedicated to the preservation of the Second Amendment. This foundation promotes the philosophy that we can no longer compromise with the gun-control fanatics. If the Second Amendment really is about freedom, then each compromise would only serve to diminish freedom a little further and ultimately give in to the establishment's incremental gun-control master plan.

It is time to end the compromising and stand firm in our preservation of the Second Amendment. The gun grabbers return each year with more and more legislative proposals, each more draconian than the previous year's.

On a more radical front, the American Justice Federation in Indianapolis, Indiana, supported the Declaration of Independence of 1994. The Federation issued an ultimatum to Congress that it initiate legislation to repeal the Fourteenth, Sixteenth and Seventeenth Amendments, the Brady Bill, the North American Free Trade Agreement and the Drug Interdiction Act, to revoke all agreements with the United Nations, to declare the federal debt to the Federal Reserve null and void, and to investigate certain actions by the various federal agencies (i.e., BATF at Waco), or be " ... brought up on charges for Treason before a court of the citizens of this Country." The ultimatum was sent by certified mail to every member of the U.S. House and Senate in April of 1994. The delivered document set a deadline for action by Congress—8:00 a.m., September 19, 1994. The Federation promised that no action taken would result in "militia units ... armed and in uniform" arriving in Washington to "arrest Congressmen who have failed to uphold their oaths of office," and seeing them "tried for Treason by Citizens' Courts."[57] The effort drew the attention of mostly disenchanted patriot groups, but the ultimatum proved fruitless.

Only the activists can determine their respective courses of activism. Some proposed actions may, at first, seem too bold for legitimate consideration, but so was drafting a Declaration of Independence from the tyrannical government of King George III. No action attracts no attention, elicits no response, results in nothing but further oppression. Passivism is more destructive than activism because it promotes continued erosion (loss) of freedom and rights. Therefore, every American citizen who still believes in the American Dream must choose his or her path of activism. From writing letters (lots of letters) to members of

---

[57] The American Justice Federation, 3850 S. Emerson Ave., Suite E, Indianapolis, IN, 46203, (317) 780-5204.

Congress to jamming up their phone and fax lines, from spreading information via phone and computer networks to joining an organized group or movement, from studying constitutional law to preparing for the day BATF agents (or United Nations' troops) appear at your door, *everyone must do something!*

Perhaps the American Justice Federation plan was premature. Mainstream America was not ready for a group of armed activists to begin placing Washington officials under citizens' arrest. An overreaction from the Justice Department would have resulted in the loss of lives, and would have presented Janet Reno with yet another opportunity to aggrandize herself to the media and left-wing leadership. Such an event would surely have spawned further restrictive legislative action in Congress detrimental to all free Americans. Perhaps the time will come when such action is absolutely warranted. However, all other avenues—public education, legislative lobbying, the voting booth, a broader united resistance by American citizens—must first be employed.

The United States Constitution was created to protect the liberty, freedom and happiness of the free citizens of the several states; it is now incumbent upon the free citizens to protect, defend and preserve the Constitution. Otherwise, you needn't worry about your gun being pried from your cold, dead fingers, because it will already have slipped from your warm, lively hands.

Fanaticism in defense of liberty is no vice.

—Senator Barry Goldwater

Our Constitution is hanging by a thread. It is our right, it is our DUTY, to make sure the tenets of freedom as proclaimed by our Founding Fathers "shall not perish from the earth."

—Richard I. Mack

One Nation Under God

On May 30, 1994, the *Donahue* television talk show presented a debate on gun control. During the discussion, a member of the audience made a comment that the right to keep and bear arms was a good idea 200 years ago because "the Redcoats were coming," but today the concept is "antiquated."

Any American so arrogant and presumptuous as to suggest the Bill of Rights, the Constitution, and/or the Declaration of Independence are antiquated should also believe *air* is antiquated, and, therefore, humankind should start looking for something else to *breathe.*

The monstrous problems of crime, drug abuse, violence and mainstream politics are evidence that our country has strayed way off course. The answers to these and other societal problems of today will not be found by charting new paths, but rather by returning to the path established by our Founding Fathers. We, as a republic, must return and never stray from the fundamental principles of liberty with which we were *"... endowed by [our] Creator."*[58] Principles of freedom do not change with time, nor because our cities have grown larger.

---

[58] The Declaration of Independence.

Our right to freedom comes only from God. How can freedom be secured and protected if we forget or ignore the Creator, who gave us liberty in the first place?

A piece of propaganda pervasive in our country is the perceived separation of church and state. Politicians and members of the media commonly quote a so-called constitutional requirement for the "separation of church and state." This statement is not found anywhere in the U.S. Constitution.

The Constitution does make two references to religion. One which requires governmental officials to be bound by oath to support the Constitution ("... *no religious test shall ever be required.*"),[59] and the other, that "... *Congress shall make no law respecting an establishment of religion, or prohibiting the free exercise thereof.*"[60]

How could any reasonable person possibly construe these two constitutional references to religion to include a requirement for separating religious principles from government? To the contrary, "The founders of the constitution wanted it clearly understood that the universal, self-evident truths of religion were fundamental to the whole structure of the American system."[61]

It should not be forgotten that the Founding Fathers believed religious precepts and morality were cornerstones of our free government. Samuel Adams warned, "Neither the wisest constitution nor the wisest laws will secure the liberty of a people whose manners are universally corrupt."[62]

---

[59] U.S. Constitution, Article VI.

[60] U.S. Constitution, Bill of Rights, First Amendment.

[61] *The Making of America*, W. Cleon Skousen, National Center for Constitutional Studies, Washington, DC, 1985, p. 675.

[62] *The Making of America*, Skousen, p. 53.

It is wholly impossible to separate the principles of freedom from the principles of religion. The God who gave us life also gave us liberty. The founders of this great country were inspired by Him to form our Constitution. President George Washington said in his farewell address, "Of all the dispositions and habits which lead to political prosperity, religion and morality are indispensable supports."[63]

The First Amendment warning to government to not make a *"law respecting an establishment of religion, or prohibiting the free exercise thereof"* was intended to prohibit a recurrence of King George III's state church, in which colonists were forced to pay tithes (taxes), and to prohibit placing one denomination over another. The forces of good and evil have always been at war with each other. Is there a deliberate effort underway to turn us off the intended path of morality and freedom by promoting a myth that the U.S. Constitution requires a separation of church and state?

Daniel Webster described the founders' traditional goal when he spoke at the New York Historical Society on February 22, 1852: "Unborn ages and visions of glory crowd upon my soul, the realization of all which, however, is in the hands and good pleasure of almighty God; but, under his divine blessing, it will be dependent on the character and virtues of ourselves and of our posterity. ... If we and they shall live always in the fear of God, and shall respect His commandments ... we may have the highest hopes of the future fortunes of our country. ... It will have no decline or fall. It will go on prospering. ... But if we and

---

[63] *The Making of America*, Skousen, p. 676.

our posterity reject religious instruction and authority, violate the rules of eternal justice, trifle with the injunctions of morality, and recklessly destroy the political constitution which holds us together, no man can tell how sudden a catastrophe may overwhelm us, that shall bury all our glory in profound obscurity. Should that catastrophe happen, let it have no history! Let the horrible narrative never be written!"[64]

Sadly and finally, if our modern American "leadership" fails to recognize that all their millions of laws, regulations, taxes and other governmental meddling are pushing our country farther off the charted course, and if we as citizens do not *demand* a return to fundamental beliefs in God, morality and freedom, then the "horrible narrative" is already being written.

The End

---

[64] *The Making of America*, Skousen, p. 688.

Duty is ours. Results are God's.

—John Quincy Adams

From My Cold Dead Fingers

Any right or freedom not worth fighting for is but a temporary privilege.

—Richard I. Mack

Afterword: "To Uphold and Defend"

An Open Letter to Fellow Police Officers
from Sheriff Richard I. Mack

This is dedicated to those brave men and women who have chosen to "protect and serve" as their vocations in life. It is written with the hope that each peace officer will seriously reflect on his and her oath of office, and rededicate him or herself to the constitutional principles upon which our country was founded and of which all police have sworn an oath to defend.

After the Revolutionary War and the subsequent creation of the U.S. Constitution, attempts to protect our newly acquired liberties were established. Certain "guards" were put in place to ensure this protection for the people. Thus began the honorable station of police service.

"I do solemnly swear that I will faithfully discharge the duties of my office, and that I will uphold and defend the Constitution of the United States from all enemies, foreign and domestic, so help me God." These, or similar, words are sworn by every police officer, public servant and government official in the entire United States. This oath carries with it a tremendous responsibility: to uphold and defend the principles of liberty for which hundreds of thousands of Americans have given their lives.

Yet, after the swearing-in ceremony, police academy graduates give little attention to the Constitution. Most police officers have never read the document they have sworn in the name of

God to uphold and defend. Most police departments and academies provide no training whatsoever regarding the Constitution. They teach their trainees to read suspects the Miranda warning, and why police cannot kick in doors whenever they feel like it. But constitutional basics are seldom included in any kind of police training. If "ignorance of the law is no excuse" for civilians, then the same should hold true for the police. Does the oath require our police to follow the Constitution, or just follow orders?

It is necessary and vital that police learn survival techniques, case law, pursuit driving, marksmanship, and so on. However, none of these is more important than the officer keeping his or her oath of office. Police must be constantly reminded (yes, through police training) why they exist and what their constitutional responsibilities are. How in God's name can basics be ignored and still full adherence to principles achieved? Police must be constitutional converts.

The precious rights secured in the U.S. Constitution have been entrusted to police for safekeeping. Police must never forget the time spent and the price paid to obtain our liberty. They can never relax the fervor with which it must be defended. How do "We the people of the United States ... secure the blessings of liberty to ourselves and our posterity" without the nation's police being dedicated to that end?

Today, police are being asked (or ordered) to enforce "laws" that clearly violate constitutional rights. Officers have been trained and inculcated to follow orders, and that police are not to interpret laws, just enforce them. That kind of military obedience has led in some cases to officers beating or shooting innocent people, confiscating property and homes, kicking in doors, writing citations with ridiculous "excessive fines," and conducting background checks on law-abiding citizens who merely wish to own a gun.

No police officer, soldier, or any other government official, should in any manner comply with an order that is unlawful or attempt to enforce a mandate that is unconstitutional. The U.S. Constitution is the supreme law of the land,[65] and it supersedes all other legislation. Police officers and soldiers can be disciplined for insubordination when they have failed to obey a *lawful* order. If the order is proved to be unlawful or unconstitutional, however, the officer or soldier cannot be disciplined for failing to obey it. In the landmark case *Miranda v. Arizona*, Chief Justice Warren wrote: "Where rights secured by the Constitution are involved, there can be no rule making or legislation which would abrogate them."

Theophilus Parsons, a Founding Father and former Chief Justice of the Massachusetts Supreme Court, wrote: "The people themselves have it in their power effectually to resist usurpation without being driven to an appeal to arms. An act of usurpation is not obligatory; it is not law and any man may be justified in his resistance." Any citizen has the right to resist an unlawful arrest, and no peace officer has a duty to make one.

Police *"... and all executive and judicial officers, both of the United States and of the several states, shall be bound by oath or affirmation to support this Constitution."*[66] Law enforcement officers are required by the Constitution to take an oath of office, and no authority exists to break that oath—not even an excuse like "following orders" of a superior.

---

[65] U.S. Constitution, Article VI, paragraph 2.

[66] U.S. Constitution, Article VI, paragraph 3.

Why would the Constitution require all police officers, all legislators, all elected officials and all public servants to swear an oath to *"defend this Constitution?"* The Founders intended that every level of government—those who make the laws, interpret the laws, enforce the laws—should have one common objective and primary purpose: to protect the individual and constitutional rights of each citizen. For that reason, every sheriff, chief of police and federal law enforcement administrator has a duty and responsibility to provide constitutional training to the officers in his or her department.

It's worth noting that a major difference exists here between being supervised by someone and working for someone. A police officer is supervised by his sergeant, captain, sheriff or chief, but every officer *works for the people.* A vast majority of Americans, and most police officers, want law and order. Together, then, the people and the police should be working to better understand the U.S. Constitution from its historical perspective.

There's no room in police work for "teaching this jerk a lesson" or "showing that guy who's boss." It serves no purpose whatsoever for police to embroil themselves in power struggles with the public. In cases where it has happened, police spend more time saving face than saving lives. Pride is a luxury police can ill afford. It merely becomes a stumbling block in their mission to protect the rights of the American people. But far too often, police officers and prosecutors become more concerned with "winning the case" than with truth and justice.

The people of the cities, towns and countrysides of America should be secure in the knowledge that the police will leave them alone if they have not broken the law or jeopardized the safety of others. The absence of unreasonable police harassment, checks and searches, is the right "to be secure in their persons, houses, papers and effects ... ."[67] It's a definition for "freedom."

It is time "... this nation, under God, shall have a new birth of freedom ..."[68] It's time for law enforcement officers to get back to the basics of law enforcement for which their jobs were created preserving our Constitution.

Police have a difficult and thankless job. They put their lives on the line every day in a world affected by drugs and violence and social decay. May each of us in this most noble profession, as we pursue the guilty among us, never be guilty ourselves of the greater crime: violating our oath in God's name to defend the constitutional rights of the people for whom we work.

Sincerely,

Sheriff Richard I. Mack
Graham County, Arizona

---

[67] U.S. Constitution, Fourth Amendment.
[68] Gettysburg Address, Abraham Lincoln, 1863.

In-text Graphs

Bibliography

Blackstone, William, *Commentaries on the Laws of England*, I, (Chicago, IL; University of Chicago Press, 1979 reprint)

Borden, Morton, *The Antifederalist Papers*, (East Lansing, MI; Michigan State University Press)

Fletcher, George P., *A Crime of Self Defense*, (New York, NY; The Free Press, A Division of Macmillan, Inc., 1988)

Kleck, Gary, *Point Blank: Guns and Violence in America*, (Hawthorne, NY; Aldine de Gruyter, 1991)

Kopel, David, *The Samurai, the Mountie, and the Cowboy: Should America Adopt the Gun Controls of Other Democracies?*, (Buffalo, NY; Prometheus Books, 1992)

LeSuer, Stephen C., *The 1838 Mormon War in Missouri*, (Columbia, MO; University of Missouri Press, 1987)

Skousen, W. Cleon, *The Making of America*, (Washington, DC; National Center for Constitutional Studies, 1985)

Suefeld, P., and Tetlock, P., eds., *Psychology and Social Advocacy*, (New York, NY; Hemisphere Press, 1990)

Index

For additional copies of this book,
quantity discount pricing,
or copies of Richard Mack's other books;
or to schedule a speaking engagement;
please call Richard Mack at:

(801) 373-0086

Or write to:

Richard I. Mack
1058 Slate Canyon Drive
Provo, UT 84606

Copies of this book
can also be purchased from
Richard Mack's web site at:

www.umedia.com/mack

or from Gun Owners of America at:

(703) 321-8585